Congressional Research Service

F-35 Joint Strike Fighter (JSF) Program

Jeremiah Gertler
Specialist in Military Aviation

February 16, 2012

Congressional Research Service

7-5700

www.crs.gov

RL30563

CRS Report for Congress ———————————

Prepared for Members and Committees of Congress

Summary

The largest procurement program in the Department of Defense (DOD), the F-35 Joint Strike Fighter (JSF), also called the Lightning II, is a new aircraft being procured in different versions for the United States Air Force, Marine Corps, and Navy. Current DOD plans call for acquiring a total of 2,456 JSFs. Hundreds of additional F-35s are expected to be purchased by several U.S. allies, eight of which are cost-sharing partners in the program.

The F-35 promises significant advances in military capability. Like many high-technology programs before it, reaching that capability has put the program above its original budget and behind the planned schedule.

The Administration's proposed FY2013 defense budget requested about $5.8 billion in procurement funding for the F-35 Joint Strike Fighter (JSF) program. This would fund the procurement of 19 F-35As for the Air Force, 6 F-35Bs for the Marine Corps, and 4 F-35Cs for the Navy.

FY2012 defense authorization act: The report on the House-passed version of the FY2011 defense authorization bill included language limiting expenditure of funds for performance improvements to the F-35 propulsion system unless development and production of such propulsion system is done competitively. Other language required the Secretary of Defense to preserve and store government-owned property acquired under the F136 propulsion system development contract and allows the contractor to conduct research, development, test, and evaluation of the F136 engine at the contractor's expense. The Senate Armed Services Committee report required that the fifth F-35 low-rate initial production contract lot be a fixed price contract, and that the contractor assume full responsibility for costs under the contract above the target cost specified in the contract. The Senate report also required DOD to implement the requirements of the Weapon Systems Acquisition Reform Act of 2009 in the F-35 program. These provisions, less the language regarding allowing the F136 contractor to continue development, and with a required report on the status of F-35B development, were included in the final conference report.

FY2012 DOD appropriations bill: The House Appropriations Committee funded 19 F-35As, 6 F-35Bs, and 7 F-35Cs, as requested, while cutting $55 million from F-35C and $75 million from F-35 research and development. The Senate Appropriations Committee funded 17 F-35As, 6 F-35Bs, and 6 F-35Cs. With cuts to R&D and advance procurement, the SAC mark funded $695 million less than the Administration request.

The conference report on FY2012 defense appropriations funded F-35 procurement at $5.9 billion for 31 aircraft (19 F-35As, 6 F-35Bs, and 7 F-35Cs), plus $455 million in advance procurement.

Contents

Tables

Appendixes

Contacts

Introduction

In General

The F-35 Joint Strike Fighter (JSF), also called the Lightning II, is a new aircraft being procured in different versions for the Air Force, Marine Corps, and Navy. The F-35 program is DOD's largest weapon procurement program in terms of total estimated acquisition cost. Current Department of Defense (DOD) plans call for acquiring a total of 2,456 JSFs[1] for the Air Force, Marine Corps, and Navy at an estimated total acquisition cost (as of December 31, 2010) of about $271 billion in constant (i.e., inflation-adjusted) FY2002 dollars. Hundreds of additional F-35s are expected to be purchased by several U.S. allies, eight of which are cost-sharing partners in the program.

The Administration's proposed FY2013 defense budget requested a total of about $9.2 billion for the F-35 program, including about $2.7 billion in Air Force and Navy research and development funding and about $6.4 billion in Air Force and Navy procurement funding. (Development and procurement of Marine Corps aircraft are funded through the Navy's budget.) The Administration proposed to fund the procurement of 19 F-35As for the Air Force, 6 F-35Bs for the Marine Corps, and 4 F-35Cs for the Navy in FY2013.

Alternate Engine Program

A long-standing debate over whether the F-35 program should include funding for an alternate engine was resolved on December 2, 2011, when the General Electric-Rolls Royce Fighter Engine Team discontinued its bid to provide an alternate engine.

Introductory information on the F-35 alternate engine program is presented in the "Background" section of this report. Due to the significance of these issues and the pace of developments, the alternate engine debate is addressed separately in CRS Report R41131, *F-35 Alternate Engine Program: Background and Issues for Congress*.

Background

The F-35 in Brief

In General

The F-35 was conceived as a relatively affordable fifth-generation strike fighter[2] that could be procured in three highly common versions for the Air Force, the Marine Corps, and the Navy, in

---

[1] Thirteen of the aircraft will be acquired for flight testing through research and development funding.

[2] Fifth-generation aircraft incorporate the most modern technology, and are considered to be generally more capable than earlier-generation aircraft. Fifth-generation fighters combine new developments such as thrust vectoring, composite materials, supercruise (the ability to cruise at supersonic speeds without using engine afterburners), stealth technology, advanced radar and sensors, and integrated avionics to greatly improve pilot situational awareness.

(continued...)

order to avoid the higher costs of developing, procuring, and operating and supporting three separate tactical aircraft designs to meet the services' similar but not identical operational needs.[3]

All three versions of the F-35 will be single-seat aircraft with the ability to go supersonic for short periods and advanced stealth characteristics. The three versions will vary somewhat in their combat ranges and payloads (see **Appendix B**). All three are to carry their primary weapons internally to maintain a stealthy radar signature. Additional weapons can be carried externally on missions requiring less stealth.

DOD states that the F-35 program "was structured from the beginning to be a model of acquisition reform, with an emphasis on jointness, technology maturation and concept demonstrations, and early cost and performance trades integral to the weapon system requirements definition process."[4]

Three Service Versions

From a common airframe and powerplant core, the F-35 is being procured in three distinct versions tailored to the needs of each military service. Differences among the aircraft include the manner of takeoff and landing, fuel capacity, and carrier suitability, among others.

Air Force CTOL Version (F-35A)

The Air Force is procuring the F-35A, a conventional takeoff and landing (CTOL) version of the aircraft. F-35As are to replace Air Force F-16 fighters and A-10 attack aircraft, and possibly F-15 fighters.[5] The F-35A is intended to be a more affordable complement to the Air Force's new F-22 Raptor air superiority fighter.[6] The F-35A is not quite as stealthy[7] nor as capable in air-to-air

---

(...continued)

Among fighters currently in service or in regular production, only the Air Force F-22 air superiority fighter and the F-35 are considered fifth-generation aircraft. Russia has flown a prototype fifth-generation fighter, and China reportedly has fifth-generation fighters under development. Regarding Russia's fifth-generation fighter project, see, inter alia, Tony Halpin, "Russia unveils its first stealth fighter jet - the Sukhoi T-50," *TimesOnline*, January 29, 2010; and Alexei Komarov, "More Sukhoi T-50s To Fly In Next 12 Months," *Aviation Week & Space Technology,* March 12, 2010. Regarding China's fifth-generation fighter project, see, inter alia, David A. Fulghum, "China Revs Up Pursuit Of Stealth Technology," *Aerospace Daily & Defense Report*, November 20, 2009; and Ted Parsons, "China's Fifth-Generation Fighter To Fly 'Soon,'" *Jane's Defence Weekly*, November 12, 2009.

Strike fighters are dual-role tactical aircraft that are capable of both air-to-ground (strike) and air-to-air (fighter) combat operations.

[3] The program's operational requirements call for 70% to 90% commonality between all three versions. Many of the three versions' high-cost components—including their engines, avionics, and major airframe structural components—are common.

Secretary of Defense William Cohen stated in 2000 that the JSF's joint approach "avoids the three parallel development programs for service-unique aircraft that would have otherwise been necessary, saving at least $15 billion." (Letter from Secretary of Defense William S. Cohen to Rep. Jerry Lewis, June 22, 2000. The text of letter made available by *Inside the Air Force* on June 23, 2000.)

[4] Department of Defense. *Selected Acquisition Report (SAR)[for] F-35 (JSF)*, December 31, 2007, p. 4.

[5] Stephen Trimble, "Lockheed says F-35s will replace USAF F-15s," *Flight International*, February 4, 2010.

[6] For more on the F-22 program, see CRS Report RL31673, *Air Force F-22 Fighter Program: Background and Issues for Congress*.

[7] A November 13, 2009, press article states that "The F-22 had a -40dBsm all-aspect reduction requirement [i.e., a requirement to reduce the radar reflectivity of the F-22 when viewed from all angles by 40 decibels per square meter], (continued...)

---

combat as the F-22, but it is more capable in air-to-ground combat than the F-22, and more stealthy than the F-16. If the F-15/F-16 combination represented the Air Force's earlier-generation "high-low" mix of air superiority fighters and more-affordable dual-role aircraft, the F-22/F-35A combination might be viewed as the Air Force's intended future high-low mix.[8] The Air Force states that "The F-22A and F-35 each possess unique, complementary, and essential capabilities that together provide the synergistic effects required to maintain that margin of superiority across the spectrum of conflict.... Legacy 4th generation aircraft simply cannot survive to operate and achieve the effects necessary to win in an integrated, anti-access environment."[9]

Marine Corps STOVL Version (F-35B)

The Marine Corps is procuring the F-35B, a short takeoff and vertical landing (STOVL) version of the aircraft.[10] F-35Bs are to replace Marine Corps AV-8B Harrier vertical/short takeoff and landing attack aircraft and Marine Corps F/A-18A/B/C/D strike fighters, which are CTOL aircraft. The Marine Corps decided to not procure the newer F/A-18E/F strike fighter[11] and instead wait for the F-35B in part because the F/A-18E/F is a CTOL aircraft, and the Marine Corps prefers aircraft capable of vertical operations. The Department of the Navy states that "The Marine Corps intends to leverage the F-35B's sophisticated sensor suite and very low observable (VLO), fifth generation strike fighter capabilities, particularly in the area of data collection, to support the Marine Air Ground Task Force (MAGTF) well beyond the abilities of today's strike and EW [electronic warfare] assets."[12]

(...continued)

while the F-35 came in at -30dBsm with some gaps in coverage." (David A. Fulghum and Bradley Perrett, "Experts Doubt Chinese Stealth Fighter Timeline," *Aerospace Daily & Defense Report*, November 13, 2009, pp. 1-2.)

[8] The term high-low mix refers to a force consisting of a combination of high-cost, high-capability aircraft and lower-cost, more-affordable aircraft. Procuring a high-low mix is a strategy for attempting to balance the goal for having a minimum number of very high capability tactical aircraft to take on the most challenging projected missions and the goal of being able to procure tactical aircraft sufficient in total numbers within available resources to perform all projected missions.

[9] Department of the Air Force Presentation to the House Armed Services Committee Subcommittee on Air and Land Forces, United States House of Representatives, Subject: Air Force Programs, Combined Statement of: Lieutenant General Daniel J. Darnell, Air Force Deputy Chief Of Staff For Air, Space and Information Operations, Plans And Requirements (AF/A3/5) [and] Lieutenant General Mark D. Shackelford, Military Deputy, Office of the Assistant Secretary of the Air Force for Acquisition (SAF/AQ) Lieutenant General Raymond E. Johns, Jr., Air Force Deputy Chief of Staff for Strategic Plans And Programs (AF/A8) May 20, 2009, pp. 7-8, 10.

[10] To permit STOVL operations, the F-35B has an engine exhaust nozzle at the rear than can swivel downward, and a mid-fuselage lift fan connected to the engine that blows air downward to help lift the forward part of the plane.

[11] For more on the F/A-18E/F program, see CRS Report RL30624, *Navy F/A-18E/F and EA-18G Aircraft Program.*

[12] Statement of Vice Admiral David Architzel, USN, Principal Military Deputy, Research, Development and Acquisition, LTGEN George J. Trautman III, USMC, Deputy Commandant for Aviation, [and] RADM Allen G. Myers, USN, Director of Warfare Integration, Before the Seapower and Expeditionary Warfare [sic: Forces] Subcommittee of the House Armed Services Committee [hearing] on [the] Department of the Navy's Aviation Procurement Program, May 19, 2009, pp. 1-2.

Navy Carrier-Suitable Version (F-35C)

The Navy is procuring the F-35C, a carrier-suitable CTOL version of the aircraft.[13] The F-35C is also known as the "CV" version of the F-35, as CV is the naval designation for aircraft carrier. The Navy plans in the future to operate carrier air wings featuring a combination of F/A-18E/Fs (which the Navy has been procuring since FY1997) and F-35Cs. The F/A-18E/F is generally considered a fourth-generation strike fighter.[14] The F-35C is to be the Navy's first aircraft designed for stealth, a contrast with the Air Force, which has operated stealthy bombers and fighters for decades. The F/A-18E/F, which is less expensive to procure than the F-35C, incorporates a few stealth features, but the F-35C is stealthier. The Department of the Navy states that "the commonality designed into the joint F-35 program will minimize acquisition and operating costs of Navy and Marine Corps tactical aircraft, and allow enhanced interoperability with our sister Service, the United States Air Force, and the eight partner nations participating in the development of this aircraft."[15]

Alternate Engine Program Summary

The F-35 is powered by the Pratt and Whitney F135 engine, which was derived from the F-22's Pratt and Whitney F119 engine. The F135 is produced in Pratt and Whitney's facilities in East Hartford and Middletown, CT.[16] Rolls-Royce is a subcontractor to Pratt and Whitney for the vertical lift system for the F-35B.

Consistent with congressional direction for the FY1996 defense budget, DOD established a program to develop an alternate engine for the F-35. The alternate engine, the F136, is being developed by a team consisting of GE Transportation—Aircraft Engines of Cincinnati, OH, and Rolls-Royce PLC of Bristol, England, and Indianapolis, IN. The F136 is a derivative of the F120 engine originally developed to compete with the F119 engine for the F-22 program.

DOD included the F-35 alternate engine program in its proposed budgets through FY2006, although Congress in certain years increased funding for the program above the requested amount and/or included bill and report language supporting the program.

The George W. Bush Administration proposed terminating the alternate engine program in FY2007, FY2008, and FY2009. The Obama Administration did likewise in FY2010. Congress rejected these proposals and provided funding, bill language, and report language to continue the program.[17]

---

[13] Features for carrier suitability include, among other things, strengthened landing gear, a strengthened airframe, and an arresting hook so as to permit catapult launches and arrested landings, as well as folding wing tips for more compact storage aboard ship.

[14] Some F/A-18E/F supporters argue that it is a "fourth-plus" or "4.5"generation strike fighter because it incorporates some fifth-generation technology, particularly in its sensors.

[15] Statement of Vice Admiral David Architzel, USN, Principal Military Deputy, Research, Development and Acquisition, LTGEN George J. Trautman III, USMC, Deputy Commandant for Aviation, [and] RADM Allen G. Myers, USN, Director of Warfare Integration, before the Seapower and Expeditionary Warfare [sic: Forces] Subcommittee of the House Armed Services Committee [hearing] on [the] Department of the Navy's Aviation Procurement Program, May 19, 2009, p. 1.

[16] Pratt and Whitney's parent firm is United Technologies.

[17] Bill language since FY2007 includes Section 211 of the FY2007 defense authorization act (H.R. 5122/P.L. 109-364 (continued...)

The General Electric/Rolls Royce Fighter Engine Team ended their effort to provide an alternate engine on December 2, 2011.

Fuller details of the alternate engine program and issues for Congress arising from it are detailed in CRS Report R41131, *F-35 Alternate Engine Program: Background and Issues for Congress*.

Recent Developments

Significant developments since the previous edition of this report on September 29, 2011, include the following:

Quick-Look Report

Although it found "no fundamental design risks," a November 29, 2011, report by a DOD team identified "13 current or likely test issues of varying severity, the combined impact of which 'results in a lack of confidence' in the aircraft's 'design stability.' The issues include the Navy version's tailhook for aircraft carrier landings, the system for dumping extra fuel before landing and excessive aircraft shaking during flight."[18] The report also noted that the F-35 had "has had more retrofits and changes than planned,"[19] and that this rate of design change requests indicated "low design maturity."[20]

Cost Overrun and LRIP-5 Agreement

Costs for current lot of low-rate initial production (LRIP-4) aircraft were reported to be 7%-10% above the contract's target cost of $3.46 billion, with the government and Lockheed Martin due to split the expected overage evenly.[21] Tom Burbage, vice president of F-35 program integration for Lockheed Martin, "says the company is already working to reduce the cost of these LRIP 4 units. 'Everybody is actually feeling reasonably good about it'" he says. 'It doesn't mean that we aren't going to have any overruns, but it is within the bounds of being manageable.'"[22]

(...continued)

of October 17, 2006) and Section 213 of the FY2008 defense authorization act (H.R. 4986/P.L. 110-181 of January 28, 2008). (For the texts of these two provisions, see CRS Report R41131, *F-35 Alternate Engine Program: Background and Issues for Congress*.)

[18] Tony Capaccio, "Pentagon Urged To Consider Slowing Lockheed F-35 Purchase Plan," *Bloomberg News*, December 6, 2011.

[19] Tony Capaccio, "Panetta Supports F-35 After Report Urges Slowing Jet Purchases," *Bloomberg News*, December 8, 2011.

[20] Tony Capaccio, "Pentagon Urged To Consider Slowing Lockheed F-35 Purchase Plan," *Bloomberg News*, December 6, 2011.

[21] Tony Capaccio, "Lockheed Faces New Potential 10 Percent F-35 Overrun, U.S. Says," *Bloomberg News*, December 2, 2011. The unit cost targets are $111.6 million for the F-35A, $109.4 million for the F-35B, and $142.9 million for the F-35C. Amy Butler, "F-35 LRIP 4 Jets 7% Over Target Cost," *Aerospace Daily*, December 2, 2011.

[22] Amy Butler, "Lockheed Once Again Predicts It Will Lower F-35 Unit Cost," *Aerospace Daily*, October 3, 2011.

This followed the Senate Armed Service's Committee's refusal to approve DOD's request to reprogram funds from other programs to cover part of a $771 million cost overrun in LRIP lots 1-3.[23]

DOD and Lockheed Martin reached agreement in early December 2011 on terms for the fifth lot of low-rate initial production F-35s (LRIP-5.) Although the per-aircraft price was not revealed, the amount of cost risk to be borne by each side was reportedly a major factor in the negotiations.

F-35B Exits "Probation"

On January 20, 2012, Secretary of Defense Leon Panetta announced that the F-35B had graduated a year early from the "probationary" status it had been placed on by Panetta's predecessor, Robert Gates. Panetta stated that "the [F-35B] variant is demonstrating the kind of performance and maturity that is in line with the other two variants of the JSF."[24] Panetta did not explain what criteria were behind the change in status. Earlier, General Joseph Dunford, assistant commandant of the Marine Corps, "cited progress in fixing technical problems and said the fighter jet met 98 percent of its test points this year."[25]

Life Extensions for Alternative Aircraft

The Air Force announced plans to extend the lives of more than 300 late-model F-16s and possibly some F-15s "to fill the gap caused by delays to the Lockheed Martin F-35 Joint Strike Fighter program."[26] The Marine Corps acquired 74 retired Harrier jets from the British Royal Air Force to provide spare parts for its AV-8B fleet, which could help extend the AV-8Bs' lifetimes until the F-35B arrives in the force.[27] The Marines' top aviation officer, General Terry Robling, said that the F-35B's IOC may not occur until 2015.[28]

Testing Progress

F-35 program testing continued at an accelerated pace. "Overall, 837 test flights were completed this year through Thursday, and both the number of individual flights and total number of test points—specific tests of specific capabilities—are running about 9 percent ahead of a restructured plan set out in January by the Pentagon's F-35 Joint Program Office."[29] Two F-35Bs completed initial compatibility trials aboard USS *Wasp* (LHD 1.) "Concerns about the jet blast from the F-35B's power engine damaging the assault ships' flight decks have proved unfounded, [Marine

---

[23] Emelie Rutherford, "SASC Denies F-35 Fund Shift For Overruns," *Defense Daily*, October 18, 2011.

[24] Colin Clark, "F-35 Starts Climb To Get Back On Track; SecDef Lifts F-35B Probation," *AOL Defense*, January 20, 2012.

[25] Andrea Shalal-Esa, "Marines Bullish On Lockheed F-35 Variant," *Reuters*, November 30, 2011.

[26] Graham Warwick, "USAF To Extend Lives Of F-16s To Cover F-35 Delays," *Aerospace Daily*, November 13, 2011.

[27] Christopher P. Cavas, Vago Muradian and Andrew Chuter, "U.S. To Buy 74 British Harrier Jets," *Defense News*, November 14, 2011 and Christopher P. Cavas, "Marines Won't Fly Brit Harriers," *Marine Corps Times*, November 17, 2011.

[28] "Marine Corps F-35 Version Slips To 2015, General Says ," *Defense Daily*, September 30, 2011.

[29] Bob Cox, "Fort Worth Star-Telegram," *Despite Budget Questions, Lockheed Martin Pushing F-35 Fighter Tests*, November 5, 2011.

Commandant James] Amos said. Thus far, the analysis is showing 'shockingly negligible' impact on the ship's deck, he said."[30]

Concurrency Disparaged

Both the F-35 program manager, Admiral David Venlet, and acting Under Secretary for Acquisition, Technology and Logistics Frank Kendall recently took issue with "a fundamental assumption of the JSF business model: concurrency."[31]

> The JSF program was originally structured with a high rate of concurrency—building production model aircraft while finishing ground and flight testing—that assumed less change than is proving necessary.

> "Fundamentally, that was a miscalculation," Venlet said. "You'd like to take the keys to your shiny new jet and give it to the fleet with all the capability and all the service life they want. What we're doing is, we're taking the keys to the shiny new jet, giving it to the fleet and saying, 'Give me that jet back in the first year. I've got to go take it up to this depot for a couple of months and tear into it and put in some structural mods, because if I don't, we're not going to be able to fly it more than a couple, three, four, five years.' That's what concurrency is doing to us."[32]

Kendall went farther:

> Putting the Lockheed Martin F-35 Joint Strike Fighter into production before flight testing had started was "acquisition malpractice," acting Pentagon acquisition chief Frank Kendall told an industry group this morning at the Center for Strategic and International Studies.

> The program, Kendall said, had started with "the optimistic prediction that we were good enough at modeling and simulation that we would not find problems in flight test."

> "That was wrong, and now we are paying for that," Kendall added.[33]

Alternative Helmet Contract Awarded

BAE Systems won a contract to provide pilot helmets for the F-35 after persistent problems with the primary helmet. "The primary helmet being developed by VSI, an Elbit and Rockwell Collins joint venture, has been suffering problems with jitter in displaying data on the visor, and resolution is not high enough for its night-vision capability."[34]

---

[30] Dave Majumdar, "Service leaders defend MV-22, STOVL F-35B ," *Air Force Times*, November 2, 2011.

[31] Richard Whittle, "JSF's Build And Test Was 'Miscalculation,' Adm. Venlet Says; Production Must Slow," *AOL Defense*, December 1, 2011.

[32] Ibid.

[33] Bill Sweetman, "JSF "Acquisition Malpractice"—Pentagon Procurement Boss," *AviationWeek/Ares blog*, February 6, 2012.

[34] Robert Wall, "BAE Systems Wins F-35 Alternative Helmet Display Work," *Aerosapce Daily*, October 11, 2011.

JSF Program Origin and Milestones

The JSF program began in the early to mid-1990s.[35] Three different airframe designs were proposed by Boeing, Lockheed, and McDonnell Douglas (the last teamed with Northrop Grumman and British Aerospace.) On November 16, 1996, the Defense Department announced that Boeing and Lockheed Martin had been chosen to compete in the Concept Demonstration phase of the program, with Pratt and Whitney providing propulsion hardware and engineering support. Boeing and Lockheed were each awarded contracts to build and test-fly two aircraft to demonstrate their competing concepts for all three planned JSF variants.[36]

The competition between Boeing and Lockheed Martin was closely watched. Given the size of the JSF program and the expectation that the JSF might be the last fighter aircraft program that DOD would initiate for many years, DOD's decision on the JSF program was expected to shape the future of both U.S. tactical aviation and the U.S. tactical aircraft industrial base.

In October 2001, DOD selected the Lockheed design as the winner of the competition, and the JSF program entered the System Development and Demonstration (SDD) phase. SDD contracts were awarded to Lockheed Martin for the aircraft and Pratt and Whitney for the aircraft's engine. General Electric continued technical efforts related to the development of an alternate engine for competition in the program's production phase.

---

[35] The JSF program emerged in late 1995 from the Joint Advanced Strike Technology (JAST) program, which began in late 1993 as a result of the Clinton Administration's Bottom-Up Review (BUR) of U.S. defense policy and programs. The BUR envisaged the JAST program as a replacement for two other tactical aircraft programs that were being terminated (the A-12 program, which was intended to provide a stealthy new carrier-based attack plane to replace the Navy's aging A-6 carrier-based attack planes, and the Multi-Role Fighter, which the Air Force had considered as a replacement for its F-16 fighters).

In 1995, in response to congressional direction, a program led by the Defense Advanced Research Projects Agency (DARPA) to develop an advanced short takeoff and vertical landing (ASTOVL) aircraft was incorporated into the JAST program. This opened the way for Marine Corps and UK participation in the JAST program, since the Marine Corps and the UK were interested procuring a new STOVL aircraft to replace their aging Harrier STOVL attack aircraft. The name of the program was then changed to Joint Strike Fighter (JSF) to focus on joint development and production of a next-generation fighter/attack plane.

A Joint Operational Requirements Document for the F-35 program was issued in March 2000 and revalidated by DOD's Joint Requirements Oversight Council (JROC) in October 2001. On October 24, 2001, the Defense Acquisition Board (DAB) held a Milestone B review for the program. (Milestone B approval would permit the program to enter the SDD phase.) On October 25, 2001, the Secretary of Defense certified to Congress (in accordance with Section 212 of the FY2001 defense authorization act [H.R. 4205/P.L. 106-398 of October 30, 2000]) that the program had successfully completed the CDP exit criteria and demonstrated sufficient technical maturity to enter SDD. On October 26, 2001, the SDD contracts were awarded to Lockheed and Pratt and Whitney. A Preliminary Design Review (PDR) for the F-35 program was conducted in April 2003, and Critical Design Reviews (CDRs) were held for the F-35A, F-35B, and F-35C in February 2006 (F-35A and F-35B) and June 2007 (F-35C).

[36] Subsequent to the selection of the Boeing and Lockheed Martin designs, Boeing acquired McDonnell Douglas and merged the two firms' JSF teams.

Table 1. F-35 Variant Milestones

	First flown	In testing	Original IOC goal	Current IOC estimate
F-35A	December 15, 2006	2 @ Edwards AFB	March 2013	2016
F-35B	June 11, 2008	3 @ NAS Patuxent River	March 2012	TBD
	First hover: March 17, 2010			
F-35C	June 6, 2010	1 @ NAS Patuxent River	March 2015	2016

Source: Prepared by CRS based on press reports and DOD testimony.

As shown in **Table 1**, the first flights of an initial version of the F-35A and the F-35B occurred in the first quarter of FY2007 and the third quarter of FY2008, respectively. The first flight of a slightly improved version of the F-35A occurred on November 14, 2009.[37] The F-35C first flew on June 6, 2010.[38]

The F-35B's ability to hover, scheduled for demonstration in November, 2009, was shown for the first time on March 17, 2010.[39] The first vertical landing took place the next day.[40]

The F-35A, F-35B, and F-35C were originally scheduled to achieve Initial Operational Capability (IOC) in March 2013, March 2012, and March 2015, respectively.[41] In March, 2010, Pentagon acquisition chief Ashton Carter announced that the Air Force and Navy had reset their projected IOCs to 2016, while Marine projected IOC remained 2012.[42] Subsequently, the Marine IOC was delayed.[43]

Procurement Quantities

Planned Total Quantities

The F-35 program includes a planned total of 2,456 aircraft for the Air Force, Marine Corps, and Navy. This included 13 research and development aircraft and 2,443 production aircraft: 1,763 F-

---

[37] "First Flight," *Defense Daily*, November 23, 2009, p. 3.

[38] Graham Warwick, " JSF Carrier Variant Meets Handling Goals On First Flight," *Aerospace Daily*, June 7, 2010.

[39] Graham Warwick, "F-35B Hovers for First Time," *Aviation Week/Ares* blog, March 17, 2010.

[40] Graham Warwick, "STOVL F-35B Makes First Vertical Landing," *Aviation Week/Ares* blog, March 18, 2010.

[41] The Navy had initially accelerated its estimated IOC for the F-35C to September 2014. Andrew Tilghman, "Joint Strike Fighter Timeline Moved Up," *NavyTimes.com*, September 18, 2009. In November 2009, Lockheed announced that the first flight of an F-35C test aircraft would be delayed from the final quarter of 2009 to the first quarter of 2010. (Dan Taylor, "Navy Joint Strike Fighter Carrier Variant Test Aircraft Will Not Fly Until 2010," *Inside the Navy*, November 9, 2009.)

[42] Testimony before the Senate Armed Services Committee, March 11, 2010. "Marine Corps IOC will include 15 aircraft for training at Eglin AFB, Fla., four in an operational test and evaluation detachment and the first operational squadron of 10 in Yuma, Ariz." Amy Butler, Robert Wall, Graham Warwick and Alon Ben-David, "F-35B Achieves Vertical Landing Milestone," *AviationWeek.com*, March 23, 2010.

[43] "The U.S. Marine Corps will scrap a December 2012 target to have its version of the Lockheed Martin Corp. F-35 Joint Strike Fighter ready for combat and isn't setting a new date, the service's commandant said. 'I'm really not wringing my hands over that,' General James Amos told reporters today at the Pentagon. 'It will be when it will be.'"—Tony Capaccio, "Marines to Delay Combat-Readiness Target for F-35 Jet," Bloomberg.com, December 14, 2010.

35As for the Air Force and a total of 680 F-35Bs and Cs for the Marine Corps and Navy, with exact numbers of Bs and Cs not yet determined.[44]

Annual Quantities

DOD began procuring F-35s in FY2007. **Table 2** shows actual F-35 procurement quantities through FY2010 and requested procurement quantities for FY2011. The figures in the table do not include 13 research and development aircraft procured with research and development funding. (Quantities for foreign buyers are discussed in the next section.)

Table 2. Annual F-35 Procurement Quantities

(Figures shown are for production aircraft; table excludes 13 research and development aircraft)

FY	F-35A (USAF)	F-35B (USMC)	F-35C (Navy)	Total
2007	2	0	0	2
2008	6	6	0	12
2009	7	7	0	14
2010	10	16	4	30
2011	22	13	7	42
2012	18	6	7	31
2013 (requested)	19	6	4	29

Source: Prepared by CRS based on DOD data.

Previous DOD plans contemplated increasing the procurement rate of F-35As for the Air Force to a sustained rate of 80 aircraft per year by FY2015, and completing the planned procurement of 1,763 F-35As by about FY2034. Past DOD plans also contemplated increasing the procurement rate of F-35Bs and Cs for the Marine Corps and Navy to a combined sustained rate of 50 aircraft per year by about FY2014, and completing the planned procurement of 680 F-35Bs and Cs by about FY2025.

On February 24, 2010, Pentagon acquisition chief Ashton Carter issued an Acquisition Decision Memorandum (ADM) restructuring the program. Although the ADM did not directly address maximum production rates or when they might be achieved, it did extend the SDD phase by 13 months, and slipped full-rate production to November, 2015.[45]

---

[44] In 1996, preliminary planning estimated over 3,000 F-35s for DOD and the UK: 2,036 for the Air Force, 642 for the Marines, 300 for the U.S. Navy, and 60 for the Royal Navy. In May 1997, the QDR recommended reducing projected DOD procurement from 2,978 to 2,852: 1,763 for the Air Force, 609 for the Marines, and 480 for the Navy. (Quadrennial Defense Review Cuts Procurement in FY1999, 2000, *Aerospace Daily*, May 20, 1997, p. 280.) In 2003, the Navy reduced its planned procurement of 1,089 F-35s to 680 aircraft as part of the Navy/Marine Corps Tactical Aviation Integration Plan. (See CRS Report RS21488, *Navy-Marine Corps Tactical Air Integration Plan: Background and Issues for Congress*, by Christopher Bolkcom and Ronald O'Rourke.)

[45] *F-35 Lightning II Joint Strike Fighter (JSF) Program Restructure Acquisition Decision Memorandum (ADM)*, Under Secretary of Defense (Acquisition, Technology & Logistics), February 24, 2010.

There is a tension between reducing costs by increasing production rates and keeping up with developmental changes, which is easier with slower rates. Lockheed Martin "has been pushing hard to increase the production rate, arguing its production line is ready and it has reduced problems on the line to speed things up. Speeding up production, of course, would boost economies of scale and help lower the politically sensitive price per plane... (S)lowing production would help reduce the cost of replacing parts in jets that are being built before testing is complete, [program manager Admiral David] Venlet said."[46]

Program Management

The JSF program is jointly managed and staffed by the Department of the Air Force and the Department of the Navy. Service Acquisition Executive (SAE) responsibility alternates between the two departments. When the Air Force has SAE authority, the F-35 program director is from the Navy, and vice versa. The Air Force resumed SAE authority in April 2009.[47]

On February 1, 2010, Secretary Gates announced that the JSF program manager had been dismissed, and that the program manager position would be upgraded from a 2-star to a 3-star billet. Vice Admiral David J. Venlet was nominated to be the new program manager on March 17, 2010,[48] and confirmed by the Senate on May 7, 2010.

Cost and Funding[49]

Total Program Acquisition Cost

As of December 31, 2010, the total estimated acquisition cost (the sum of development cost, procurement cost, and military construction [MilCon] cost) of the F-35 program in constant (i.e.,

---

[46] Richard Whittle, "JSF's Build And Test Was 'Miscalculation,' Adm. Venlet Says; Production Must Slow," *AOL Defense*, December 1, 2011.

[47] In 2004, appropriations conferees followed a House recommendation to direct DOD to review this alternative management arrangement. House appropriators believed that "management of program acquisition should remain with one Service, and that the U.S. Navy, due to its significant investment in two variants of the F-35 should be assigned all acquisition executive oversight responsibilities." (H.Rept. 108-553 [H.R. 4613], p. 234) Conferees directed that DOD submit a report on the potential efficacy of this change. Prior to the release of the DOD report, former Air Force Chief of Staff General John Jumper was quoted as saying that he also supported putting one service in charge of JSF program acquisition. (Elizabeth Rees, "Jumper Supports Single Service Retaining JSF Acquisition Oversight," *Inside the Air Force*, August 6, 2004.) However, General Jumper highlighted the significant investment the Air Force was making in the JSF program in response to the congressional language favoring the Navy. In DOD's response to Congress, the report noted the current arrangement ensures one Service does not have a "disproportionate voice" when it comes to program decisions and that the current system is "responsive, efficient, and in the best interests of the success of the JSF program." (U.S. Department of Defense, *Report to Congress on Joint Strike Fighter Management Oversight* [forwarded by] Michael W. Wynne, Under Secretary of Defense for Acquisition, Technology and Logistics, December 20, 2004.)

[48] Michael Bruno, "Navy Three Star Officially Nominated For JSF," *AviationWeek.com*, March 17, 2010.

[49] The F-35 program receives (or in the past received) funding from the Air Force, Navy, and Defense-Wide research, development, test, and evaluation (RDT&E) accounts (the Defense-Wide RDT&E funding occurred in FY1996-FY1998); Non-Treasury Funds (i.e., financial contributions from the eight other countries participating in the F-35 program)—a source of additional research and development funding; the Air Force and Navy aircraft procurement accounts (the Navy and Marine Corps are organized under the Department of the Navy, and Marine Corps aircraft development and procurement costs are funded through the Navy's RDT&E and aircraft procurement accounts); and the Air Force MilCon account and the Navy and Marine Corps MilCon account.

---

inflation-adjusted) FY2002 dollars was about $270.6 billion, including about $48.4 billion in research and development, about $221.8 billion in procurement, and about $457.4 million in MilCon.[50]

In then-year dollars (meaning dollars from various years that are not adjusted for inflation), the figures are about $379.4 billion, including about $54.4 billion in research and development, about $324.4 billion in procurement, and about $551.2 million in military construction.[51]

Prior-Year Funding

Through FY2010, the F-35 program has received a total of roughly $56 billion of funding in then-year dollars, including roughly $41 billion in research and development, about 14.1 billion in procurement, and roughly $227.8 million in military construction.

Unit Costs

As of December 31, 2010, the F-35 program had a program acquisition unit cost (or PAUC, meaning total acquisition cost divided by the 2,456 research and development and procurement aircraft) of about $154.4 million in constant FY2010 dollars, and an average procurement unit cost (or APUC, meaning total procurement cost divided by the 2,443 production aircraft) of $132.8 million in constant FY2010 dollars.

LRIP IV cost

On November 19, 2010, DOD announced the award of a contract for the fourth lot of low rate initial production (LRIP) F-35s. This $3.9 billion contract for 31 aircraft is fixed-price-incentive (firm target), meaning that Lockheed Martin and the government "would equally share the burden of a cost overrun up to 40% over the fixed price. Any overage above 40% would be Lockheed's responsibility. Based on the per-unit price of roughly $126 million, the cost could go as high as about $176 million, but the price paid by the government would be capped at around $151 million."[52]

> Based on the LRIP IV contract, the target prices of the three F-35 variants without engines are as follows: conventional takeoff and landing (CTOL)—$111.6 million; Short takeoff and vertical landing (Stovl)—$109.4 million and carrier variant (CVs)—$142.9 million. Though Stovl appears to cost the least, the per-unit engine price is the highest. Also, this number is lower because the purchase includes 17 Stovls versus 11 CTOLs and only four CVs.[53]

LRIP IV has since incurred substantial overruns (see "Recent Developments" above).

---

[50] Office of the Secretary of Defense, *Selected Acquisition Report (SAR): F-35*, December 31, 2010. The procurement cost figure of about $198.4 billion does not include the cost of several hundred additional F-35s that are to be procured other countries that are participating in the F-35 program. The $198.4 billion figure does, however, assume certain production-cost benefits for DOD aircraft that result from producing F-35s for other countries.

[51] Office of the Secretary of Defense, *Selected Acquisition Report (SAR): F-35*, December 31, 2010.

[52] Amy Butler, "Lockheed Says Latest F-35 Buy Following Predicted Cost Curve," *Aerospace Daily*, December 3, 2010.

[53] Amy Butler, "Carter: Healthy JSF Development Worth A Slip In Production," *Aerospace Daily*, December 22, 2010.

Operating and Support Costs

The December 31, 2010, Selected Acquisition Report projected lifetime operating and sustainment costs for the F-35 fleet at slightly over $1 trillion.[54] Because that figure was based on experience with older fighters, it is being updated. "The Pentagon's Cost Analysis and Program Evaluation group is updating its $1 trillion figure for a major F-35 review next month intended to revise all of the program's costs ... the program office will begin a so-called baseline review of the sustainment cost, similar to the F-35 design and production review conducted last year."[55]

Deficit Reduction Commission Recommendation

On December 3, 2010, the National Commission on Fiscal Responsibility and Reform released its report on ways to decrease the United States' national debt. The commission's suggestions included canceling the F-35B outright, for a savings of $17.6 billion, and substituting F-16s and F/A-18Es for half of the planned F-35A and C purchases. The commission estimated the new fighter mix would save $9.5 billion through FY2015.[56]

Lockheed Martin chief financial officer Bruce Tanner "said the commission's proposal is currently not viable... because Lockheed Martin's Fort Worth fighter factory is now optimized for F-35 production and would only be able to build a maximum of four F-16s per month."[57]

Manufacturing Locations

Current plans call for the F-35 to be manufactured in several locations. Lockheed will build the aircraft's forward section in Fort Worth, TX. Northrop will build the mid-section in Palmdale, CA, and the tail will be built by BAE Systems in the United Kingdom. Final assembly of these components will take place in Fort Worth. Program officials are considering the potential of establishing a second final assembly and checkout facility in Italy.[58]

The Pratt and Whitney F135 engine for the F-35 is produced in East Hartford and Middletown, CT.

International Participation

In General

The F-35 program is DOD's largest international cooperative program. DOD has actively pursued allied participation as a way to defray some of the cost of developing and producing the aircraft,

---

[54] Office of the Secretary of Defense, *Selected Acquisition Report (SAR): F-35*, December 31, 2010, p. 53.

[55] Tony Capaccio, "Lockheed Martin F-35 Operating Costs May Reach $1 Trillion," *Bloomberg News*, April 21, 2011.

[56] Jim Wolf, "Lockheed F-35 fighter in US deficit panel's sights," *Reuters.com*, November 10, 2010; John T. Bennett, "U.S. Debt Panel: Cut Weapon Programs," *Defense News*, December 6, 2010.

[57] Marina Malenic, "Lockheed Martin Officials Defend F-35 As 'Affordable,'" *Defense Daily*, December 3, 2010.

[58] "Eventually [Lockheed Martin] may want to open a second production line in Italy to better match demand, said Tom Burbage, executive vice president and general manager of the F-35 program." Christopher Hinton, "Lockheed Martin sees international demand growing for F-35," *MarketWatch.com*, June 17, 2009.

and to "prime the pump" for export sales of the aircraft.[59] Allies in turn view participation the F-35 program as an affordable way to acquire a fifth-generation strike fighter, technical knowledge in areas such as stealth, and industrial opportunities for domestic firms.

Eight allied countries—the United Kingdom, Canada, Denmark, The Netherlands, Norway, Italy, Turkey, and Australia—are participating in the F-35 program under a Memorandum of Understanding (MOU) for the SDD and Production, Sustainment, and Follow-On Development (PSFD) phases of the program, although March, 2010 reports indicated Denmark may withdraw.[60] These eight countries have contributed varying amounts of research and development funding to the program, receiving in return various levels of participation in the program. International partners are also assisting with Initial Operational Test and Evaluation (IOT&E), a subset of SDD.[61] The eight partner countries are expected to purchase hundreds of F-35s, with the United Kingdom being the largest anticipated foreign purchaser.[62]

Two additional countries—Israel and Singapore—are security cooperation participants outside the F-35 cooperative development partnership.[63] Israel has agreed to purchase 20 F-35s.[64] Japan chose the F-35 as its next fighter in October 2011, and sales to additional countries are possible.[65] Some officials have speculated that foreign sales of F-35s might eventually surpass 2,000 or even 3,000 aircraft.[66]

The UK is the most significant international partner in terms of financial commitment, and the only Level 1 partner.[67] On December 20, 1995, the U.S. and UK governments signed an MOU on

---

[59] Congress insisted from the outset that the JAST program include ongoing efforts by DARPA to develop more advanced STOVL aircraft, opening the way for UK participation in the program.

[60] See, inter alia, Bill Sweetman, "Denmark bails from JSF," *Aviation Week/Ares blog*, March 15, 2010.

[61] Currently, the UK, Italy, and the Netherlands have agreed to participate in the IOT&E program. UK, the senior F-35 partner, will have the strongest participation in the IOT&E phase. Italy and the Netherlands are contributing a far smaller amount and will take part only in the coalition concept of operations (CONOPS) validation testing. (Telephone conversation with OSD/AT&L, October 3, 2007.) Other partner nations are still weighing their option to participate in the IOT&E program. The benefits to participation are expedited acquisition of aircraft, pilot training for the test cycle, and access to testing results.

[62] Debate continues in the United Kingdom over whether to base the design of its new carriers on availability of the STOVL F-35B, which would minimize the need for launch and arresting gear and a deck capable of landing CTOL aircraft, or to build them to a more conventional design. (See, inter alia, "Davies: both carriers will take JSF," *DefenseManagement.com*, November 3, 2009.)

[63] DOD offers Foreign Military Sales (FMS)-level of participation in the F-35 program for countries unable to commit to partnership in the program's SDD phase. Israel and Singapore are believed to have contributed $50 million each, and are "Security Cooperative Participants." (Selected Acquisition Report, Office of the Secretary of Defense for Acquisition. December 31, 2005.)

[64] Bob Cox, "Israeli government ok's F-35 buy," *Fort Worth Star-Telegram*, September 16, 2010. Yaakov Lappin, "Israel, US Sign F-35 Agreement," *Jerusalem Post*, October 8, 2010.

[65] Paul Kallender-Umezu, "Japan F-X Competition Win Victory for JSF Program," *Defense News*, December 20, 2011. Viola Gienger, "Pentagon Awaits India's Interest in Lockheed Martin F-35 Fighter," *Bloomberg News*, November 2, 2011.

[66] Andrea Shalal-Esa, "Pentagon sees 6,000 possible F-35 sales," *Reuters.com*, June 17, 2009. See also Marina Malenic, "F-35 Sales Could Double As Countries Look To Replace Aging Fleets, General Says," *Defense Daily*, June 18, 2009: 6, and Marcus Weisgerber, "JSF Program Anticipates Nearly 700 F-35 Buys [For International Customers] Between FY-09 and FY-23, *Inside the Air Force*, July 31, 2009.

[67] International participation in the F-35 program is divided into three levels, according to the amount of money a country contributes to the program—the higher the amount, the greater the nation's voice with respect to aircraft requirements, design, and access to technologies gained during development. Level 1 Partner status requires approximately 10% contribution to aircraft development and allows for fully integrated office staff and a national (continued...)

British participation in the JSF program as a collaborative partner in the definition of requirements and aircraft design. This MOU committed the British government to contribute $200 million toward the cost of the 1997-2001 Concept Demonstration Phase.[68] On January 17, 2001, the U.S. and UK governments signed an MOU finalizing the UK's participation in the SDD phase, with the UK committing to spending $2 billion, equating to about 8% of the estimated cost of SDD. A number of UK firms, such as BAE and Rolls-Royce, participate in the F-35 program.[69]

On October 18, 2010, the British government announced a significant revision to its F-35 acquisition. Following a major defense review, the British chose to reduce their planned buy "from 138 planes to as few as 40,"[70] and to withdraw from acquiring the F-35B short-takeoff-vertical landing model. "The British instead will buy the less costly F-35C model being developed for the U.S. Navy, and only enough planes to equip one small carrier around 2020."[71]

International Sales Quantities and Schedule

The cost of F-35s for U.S. customers depends in part on the total quantity of F-35s produced. As the program has proceeded, some new potential customers have emerged, such as South Korea and Japan, mentioned above. Other countries have considered increasing their buys, while some have deferred previous plans to buy F-35s.

(...continued)

deputy at director level.

Level II partners consist of Italy and the Netherlands, contributing $1 billion and $800 million, respectively. On June 24, 2002, Italy became the senior Level II partner ("F-35 Joint Strike Fighter (JSF) Lightning II: International Partners," http://www.globalsecurity.org/military/systems/aircraft/f-35-int htm). Italy wants to have its own F-35 final assembly line, which would be in addition to a potential F-35 maintenance and upgrade facility. The Netherlands signed on to the F-35 program on June 17, 2002, after it had conducted a 30-month analysis of potential alternatives.

Australia, Denmark, Norway, Canada, and Turkey joined the F-35 program as Level III partners, with contributions ranging from $125 million to $175 million. ("Australia, Belgium Enter Joint Strike Fighter Program as EMD Partners," *Inside the Air Force*, April 21, 2000.)

Unlike the SDD phase, PSFD phase does not make any distinction as to levels of participation. Also unlike the bilateral SDD MOUs, there is a single PSFD MOU for all partner nations. In signing the PSFD MOU, partner nations state their intentions to purchase the F-35, including quantity and variant, and a determination is made as to their delivery schedule. PSFD costs will be divided on a "fair-share" based on the programmed purchase amount of the respective nation. So-called "offset" arrangements, considered the norm in defense contracts with foreign nations, usually require additional incentives to compensate the purchasing nation for the agreement's impact to its local workforce. F-35 officials decided to take a different approach, in line with the program's goal to control costs, to avoid offset arrangements and promote competition as much as possible. Consequently, all partner nations have agreed to compete for work on a "best-value" basis and have signed the PSFD MOU.

[68] "U.S., U.K. Sign JAST Agreement," *Aerospace Daily*, December 21, 1995, p. 451.

[69] BAE is a major partner to Lockheed Martin and is providing the aft fuselage, empennage, and electronic warfare suite for the aircraft. Rolls-Royce is partnered with GE on the F136 engine and is a subcontractor to Pratt and Whitney for producing components for the F-35B's STOVL lift system. In October 2009, Rolls Royce broke ground on a new plant in Virginia to make parts for the F136 engine. (Rolls Royce press release, "Rolls-Royce expands US capability; begins construction on new manufacturing facility in Virginia," October 19, 2009, available at http://www.rolls-royce.com/investors/news/2009/091019_manufacturing_virginia.jsp.) Rolls Royce's 2001 contract with Pratt and Whitney for design and development of the STOVL lift components is valued at $1 billion over 10 years. ("Rolls-Royce Finishes First JSF Propulsion System Flight Hardware," Rolls-Royce Media Room, available at http://www.rolls-royce.com/media/showPR.jsp?PR_ID=40243.) All F-35Bs, regardless of what engine they use, are to employ Rolls Royce components in their STOVL lift systems.

[70] Bob Cox, "Great Britain to delay, trim F-35 purchases," *Fort Worth Star-Telegram*, October 20, 2010.

[71] Ibid.

The Italian government announced on February 15, 2012, that its planned buy of 131 F-35s would be reduced to 90.[72] Norway has deferred its buy by two years, to 2016.[73] The Netherlands reportedly delayed delivery of its first F-35s by four years, to 2019.[74] Canada has reduced its projected buy from 80 aircraft to 65. "'One of the reasons there will be fewer of the new fighters is we anticipate the new fighters will have significantly greater capacity than existing fighters,' Prime Minister Stephen Harper told a news conference."[75] "Defence Minister Peter MacKay, a strong advocate of the F-35, dismissed growing criticism of Canada's pledge to buy 65 of the planes as 'clatter and noise.'... Mr. MacKay said the plane is 'absolutely crucial' for the protection of North America. Later, asked if he has a plan B, he replied that no other jet is comparable."[76] On the other hand, Turkey may reportedly increase its buy from 100 to 120, and Israel from 20 to 40.[77] In the case of Australia:

> [W]ith the core U.S. program under intensive cost pressure, Australia held off until 2012 on a further commitment for 72 fighters to outfit the first three operational squadrons. By then, the government "will have much firmer cost estimates for the remaining aircraft and necessary support and enabling capability as part of the planned first multi-year buy that is expected to comprise over 1,000 aircraft for the U.S., Australia and other partners," Defense Minister John Faulkner says.[78]

Friction over Work Shares and Technology Transfer

DOD and foreign partners in the JSF program have occasionally disagreed over the issues of work shares and proprietary technology. Denmark, Italy, the Netherlands, Norway, and Turkey expressed dissatisfaction in 2003-2004 with the type and quantity of the work their companies had been awarded on the F-35.[79] These countries threatened to reduce their participation in the program, or to purchase European fighters instead of the F-35.

---

[72] Chiara Vasarri and Sabine Pirone, "Italy to Cut F-35 Fighter Jet Orders in Revamp," *Bloomberg News*, February 15, 2012.

[73] Robert Wall, "Norway Delays Most F-35 Deliveries," *Aerospace Daily*, September 28, 2010; John Reed, "Norway Buys 4 JSFs, Pitches New Missile," *DefenseTech.org*, June 21, 2011.

[74] Robert Wall, "Dutch Say JSF Delays Will Not Impact Air Force, For Now," *Aerospace Daily*, November 30, 2011.

[75] Randall Palmer and David Ljunggren, "Canada to buy fewer F-35 fighters than thought," *Reuters.com*, May 12, 2008. Daniel Leblanc, " Ottawa to spend $9-billion in sole-source deal for U.S. fighter jets," *The Globe and Mail*, June 8, 2010. See also "Canada Commits $8.5 Billion For 65 Lockheed Martin F-35s," *Defense Daily*, July 19, 2010; "Purchase Decision Allows Canada To Begin F-35 Planning," *Aerospace Daily*, July 19, 2010, and Dana Hedgpeth, "Lockheed In $9 Billion Jet Deal With Canada," *Washington Post*, July 17, 2010.

[76] Oliver Moore, "Panetta Reassures Canada: U.S. 'Committed' To F-35 Jet Program," *The Globe and Mail*, November 19, 2011.

[77] Umit Enginsoy and Burak Ege Bekdil, "Fighter Buys Top Turkish Shopping List," *Defense News*, April 28, 2008. Gopal Ratnam and Viola Gienger, "Israel Seeks 20 Additional F-35s After Failure Of U.S. Swap For Peace Plan," *Bloomberg.com*, December 14, 2010.

[78] Robert Wall, "Will Australian JSF Buy Avoid Delays?" *AviationWeek.com*, December 2, 2009. A similar story appeared in the print edition of *Aviation Week & Space Technology*, November 30, 2009.

[79] "Norway Signs Industrial Partnership with Eurofighter Consortium," *Defense Daily,* January 29, 2003. Joris Janssen Lok, "Frustration Mounts Among JSF Partners," *Jane's Defence Weekly*, March 24, 2004; Thomas Dodd, "Danish Companies Consider Quitting JSF Programme," *Jane's Defence Weekly*, January 9, 2004. Tom Kingston, "Unsatisfied Italy May Cut JSF Participation," *Defense News*, May 10, 2004. Lale Sariibrahimoglu, "Turkey may withdraw from JSF program," *Jane's Defence Weekly*, November 10, 2004.

Israel announced that it had an agreement for $5.3 billion in proposed offsets as part of its deal to acquire 20 F-35s, leading to Canadian objections that their much larger investment would yield a proportionally smaller share of offset work.[80]

The governments of Italy and the United Kingdom have lobbied for F-35 assembly facilities to be established in their countries. In July 2010, Lockheed and the Italian firm Alenia Aeronautica reached an agreement to establish an F-35 final assembly and checkout facility at Cameri Air base, Italy, to deliver aircraft for Italy and the Netherlands beginning in 2014.[81] It was also reported that South Korean companies could bid for work on the F-35 if South Korea purchases the aircraft.[82]

In November 2009, it was reported that the Confederation of Danish Industries had demanded that the Danish government secure subcontract guarantees with Lockheed regarding Danish work on the F-35 program before the Danish government makes a selection to purchase the F-35 for Denmark's Combat Aircraft Replacement Program.[83]

Some foreign partners in the F-35 program have argued that the United States has been too cautious regarding the transfer of JSF technologies. Following UK expressions in early 2006 of frustration regarding technology sharing,[84] Congress included a provision (Section 233) in the FY2007 defense authorization act (H.R. 5122/P.L. 109-364 of October 17, 2006) expressing the sense of the Congress that the Secretary of Defense should share JSF technology between the U.S. and UK governments consistent with the national security interests of both nations.[85] However, a November 24, 2009, report indicated that the Pentagon had decided not to share critical technologies with the UK.[86]

As of 2008, international content in the initial F-35 aircraft was approximately 20%, and Lockheed expected international content to potentially expand to about 30% as the program transitions to full-rate production and the supply base potentially diversifies.[87]

---

[80] Barbara Opall-Rome and David Pugliese, "Israeli Clarification Calms Canada's Ire on Offsets," *Defense News*, December 20, 2010.

[81] Amy Butler, "Deal For Italian JSF Assembly Facility Finally Set," *Aerospace Daily*, July 20, 2010.

[82] "Lockheed Martin Dangles F-35 Work Opportunities For S. Korea," *Aerospace Daily & Defense Report*, October 21, 2009: 5.

[83] Gerard O'Dwyer, "Danish Industry Pushes for F-35 Work Guarantees," *Defense News*, November 23, 2009: 23.

[84] The UK's top defense procurement official reportedly stated in 2006 that his country would cease participation in the F-35 program if the F136 engine were cancelled and technology transfer issues were not resolved to the UK's satisfaction. (Megan Scully, "British Demand Better Access To Fighter." *National Journal's Congress Daily AM*, March 15, 2006. George Cahlink. "U.K. Procurement Chief Warns Backup Engine Dispute Threatens JSF Deal." *Defense Daily*, March 15, 2006.)

[85] The text of the provision is as follows:

> SEC. 233. SENSE OF CONGRESS ON TECHNOLOGY SHARING OF JOINT STRIKE FIGHTER TECHNOLOGY.
>
> It is the sense of Congress that the Secretary of Defense should share technology with regard to the Joint Strike Fighter between the United States Government and the Government of the United Kingdom consistent with the national security interests of both nations.

[86] Jim Wolf, "U.S. to Withhold F-35 Fighter Software Code," *Reuters.com*, November 24, 2009. Rhys Jones, "UK confident U.S. will hand over F-35 fighter codes," *Reuters.com*, December 7, 2009.

[87] "F-35 International Program Content," JSF Joint Program Office paper, March 4, 2008.

Proposed FY2013 Budget

FY2013 Funding Request

Table 3 shows the Administration's FY2013 request for Air Force and Navy research and development and procurement funding for the F-35 program, along with FY2011 and FY2012 funding levels. The funding figures shown in the table do not include procurement funding for initial spares, MilCon funding, or research and development funding provided by other countries.

Table 3. FY2013 Funding Request for F-35 Program

(Figures in millions of then-year dollars; FY2011 and FY2012 figures shown for reference)

	FY2011		FY2012		FY2013 (request)	
	Funding	**Quantity**	**Funding**	**Quantity**	**Funding**	**Quantity**
RDT&E funding						
Air Force	931.6	—	1,397.9	—	1,218.4	—
Dept. of Navy	1,256.3	—	1,310.3	—	1,481.1	—
Subtotal	2,187.9	—	2,708.2	—	2,699.5	—
Procurement funding						
Air Force	4,302.2	25	3,518.6	18	3,565.7	19
Dept. of Navy	2,691.1	10	2,816.3	13	2,583.7	10
Subtotal	6,993.3	35	6,334.9	31	6,149.4	29
Spares	501.1		202.9		322.3	
TOTAL	9,682.3	35	9,246.0	31	9,171.2	29

Source: *Program Acquisition Costs by Weapons System*, Office of the Under Secretary of Defense (Comptroller)/Chief Financial Officer, February, 2012.

Notes: Figures shown do not include funding for MilCon funding or research and development funding provided by other countries. Advance procurement requested in FY2013 for future years, $293.4 million for the Air Force and $171.4 million for the Navy, is included in the procurement amounts shown.

Procurement cost of the 19 F-35As requested for FY2013 in the Air Force budget is estimated at $3,353.3 million, or an average of $176.5 million each. These aircraft have received $229.0 million in prior-year advance procurement (AP) funding, leaving another $3,124.3 million to be funded in FY2013 to complete their estimated procurement cost. The FY2013 Air Force funding request for the F-35 program also includes $293.4 million in advance procurement funding for F-35As to be procured in future years, and $181.8 million for F-35A initial spares, bringing the total FY2013 Air Force procurement funding request for the program to $3,599.5 million.

The 6 F-35Bs and 4 F-35Cs requested for FY2013 in the Department of the Navy budget have a combined estimated procurement cost of $2,638.7 million, or an average of $263.9 million each. These aircraft have received $226.3 million in prior-year AP funding, leaving another $2,412.3 million to be funded in FY2013 to complete their estimated procurement cost. The FY2013 Department of the Navy procurement funding request for the F-35 program also includes $171.4 million in advance procurement funding for F-35Bs and Cs to be procured in future years, and

$140.5 million funding for initial spares, bringing the total FY2013 Navy procurement funding request for the program to $2,724.2 million.

Issues for Congress

Planned Total Procurement Quantities

Another potential issue for Congress concerns the total number of F-35s to be procured. As mentioned above, planned production totals for the various versions of the F-35 we left unchanged by the 2010 Quadrennial Defense Review (QDR). Since then, considerable new information has appeared regarding cost growth that may challenge the ability to maintain the expected procurement quantities. "'I think we are to the point in our budgetary situation where, if there is unanticipated cost growth, we will have to accommodate it by reducing the buy,' said Undersecretary of Defense Robert Hale, the Pentagon comptroller."[88]

Some observers, noting potential limits on future U.S. defense budgets, potential changes in adversary capabilities, and competing defense-spending priorities, have suggested reducing planned total procurement quantities for the F-35. A September 2009 report on future Air Force strategy, force structure, and procurement by the Center for Strategic and Budgetary Assessments (CSBA), for example, states that

> [A]t some point over the next two decades, short-range, non-stealthy strike aircraft will likely have lost any meaningful deterrent and operational value as anti-access/area denial systems proliferate. They will also face major limitations in both irregular warfare and operations against nuclear-armed regional adversaries due to the increasing threat to forward air bases and the proliferation of modern air defenses. At the same time, such systems will remain over-designed – and far too expensive to operate – for low-end threats....
>
> Reducing the Air Force plan to buy 1,763 F-35As through 2034 by just over half, to 858 F-35As, and increasing the [annual F-35A] procurement rate to end [F-35A procurement] in 2020 would be a prudent alternative. This would provide 540 combat-coded F-35As on the ramp, or thirty squadrons of F-35s[,] by 2021[, which would be] in time to allow the Air Force budget to absorb other program ramp ups[,] like NGB [the next-generation bomber].[89]

Program Performance

The F-35 program is behind schedule and over budget. Congress may wish to review the causes of these issues, whether the plan put forward in February 2010 and subsequent procurement delay in February 2012 are sufficient to recover schedule and stabilize costs, and/or the credibility of projections by DOD, GAO, and others regarding the program's likely future performance.

---

[88] Marina Malenic, "DoD Comptroller: Further F-35 Cost Growth Jeopardizes Buy Quantity," *Defense Daily*, March 4, 2010.

[89] Thomas P. Ehrhard, *An Air Force Strategy for the Long Haul*, Washington, Center for Strategic and Budgetary Assessments, 2009, pp. xii and xiv. The report was released on September 17, 2009, according to CSBA's website, and is available at http://www.csbaonline.org/4Publications/PubLibrary/R.20090917.An_Air_Force_Strat/R.20090917.An_Air_Force_Strat.pdf. Subsequent to writing this report, the author became a special assistant to the Air Force Chief of Staff.

Cost Increases and Nunn-McCurdy Breach

On March 20, 2010, DOD formally announced that the JSF program had exceeded the cost increases limits specified in the Nunn-McCurdy cost containment law, as average procurement unit cost, in FY2002 dollars, had grown 57% to 89% over the original program baseline. Simply put, this requires the Secretary of Defense to notify Congress of the breach, present a plan to correct the program, and to certify that the program is essential to national security before it can continue.[90]

> On June 2, 2010, the Under Secretary of Defense for Acquisition, Technology and Logistics issued an Acquisition Decision Memorandum (ADM) certifying the F-35 Program in accordance with section 2433a of title 10, United States Code. As required by section 2433a, of title 10, Milestone B was rescinded. A Defense Acquisition Board (DAB) was held in November 2010... No decision was rendered at the November 2010 DAB... Currently, cumulative cost and schedule pressures result in a critical Nunn-McCurdy breach to both the original (2001) and current (2007) baseline for both the Program Acquisition Unit Cost (PAUC) and Average Procurement Unit Cost (APUC). The breach is currently reported at 78.23% for the PAUC and 80.66% for the APUC against the original baseline and 27.34% for the PAUC and 31.23% for the APUC against the current baseline.[91]

This breach led to the January 2011 program restructuring described in "Recent Developments."

February 2010 Program Restructuring

In November 2009, DOD's Joint Estimating Team issued a report (JET II) stating that the F-35 program would need an extra 30 months to complete the SDD phase. In response to JET II, the then-impending Nunn-McCurdy breach and other developments, on February 24, 2010, Pentagon acquisition chief Ashton Carter issued an Acquisition Decision Memorandum (ADM) restructuring the F-35 program. Key elements of the restructuring included the following:

- Extending the SDD phase by 13 months, thus delaying Milestone C (full-rate production) to November 2015 and adding an extra low-rate initial production (LRIP) lot of aircraft to be purchased during the delay. Carter proposed to make up the difference between JET II's projected 30-month delay and his 13-month schedule by adding three extra early-production aircraft to the test program. It is not clear how extra aircraft could be added promptly if production is already behind schedule.

- Funding the program to the "Revised JET II" (13-month delay) level, implicitly accepting the JET II findings as valid.

- Withholding $614 million in award fees from the contractor for poor performance, while adding incentives to produce more aircraft than planned within the new budget.

[90] For a history of the Nunn-McCurdy law and options for its future, see CRS Report R41293, *The Nunn-McCurdy Act: Background, Analysis, and Issues for Congress*, by Moshe Schwartz.

[91] Office of the Secretary of Defense, *Selected Acquisition Report (SAR): F-35*, December 31, 2010, p. 4.

- Moving procurement funds to R&D. "More than $2.8 billion that was budgeted earlier to buy the military's next-generation fighter would instead be used to continue its development."[92]

"Taken together, these forecasts result in the delivery of 122 fewer aircraft over the Future Years Defense Program (FYDP), relative to the President's FY 2010 budget baseline," Carter said.[93] This reduction led the Navy and Air Force to revise their dates for IOC as noted above.

February 2012 Procurement Stretch

With the FY2013 budget, F-35 acquisition was slowed, with the acquisition of 179 previously planned aircraft being moved to years beyond the FY2013-2017 FYDP "2017 for a total of $15.1 billion in savings."[94]

OT&E Report on System Testing

In its annual report to Congress on DOD programs, the Office of Operational Testing & Evaluation (DOT&E) stated that due to late deliveries of 10 of 13 test aircraft, F-35 flight testing "accomplished only 16 of 168 flight test sorties planned for FY09," and characterized the test plan as having substantial schedule risk. While giving credit for "a comprehensive, robust, and fully funded Live Fire test plan," DOT&E also noted "the removal of shutoff fuses for engine fueldraulics lines, coupled with the prior removal of dry bay fire extinguishers [to save weight], has increased the likelihood of aircraft combat losses from ballistic threat induced fires."[95]

March 2010 GAO Perspective

In March 2010, the Government Accountability Office (GAO) issued a report reviewing the F-35 program's cost, schedule, and performance. Citing what it found to be deficiencies in the manufacturing process and test schedule, and noting the high level of concurrency in the program, GAO found that "JSF cost increases, schedule delays, and continuing technical problems ... increase the risk that the program will not be able to deliver the aircraft quantities and capabilities in the time required by the warfighter."[96] DOD concurred with GAO's recommendations concerning independent cost analysis and review of IOC requirements, noting that DOD had already taken corrective actions (such as the program restructuring) in advance of GAO's report, and partially concurred with a recommendation to move toward fixed-price contracting.[97]

---

[92] Tony Capaccio, "Lockheed F-35 Purchases Delayed in Pentagon's Fiscal 2011 Plan," *Bloomberg News*, January 6, 2010.

[93] *F-35 Lightning II Joint Strike Fighter (JSF) Program Restructure Acquisition Decision Memorandum (ADM)*, Under Secretary of Defense (Acquisition, Technology & Logistics), February 24, 2010.

[94] Tony Capaccio, "Pentagon Takes $1.6 Billion From Lockheed F-35 in Biggest Cut," *Bloomberg News*, February 13, 2012.

[95] DOD Office of Operational Test & Evaluation, *FY2009 DOT&E Annual Report to Congress*, pp. 21-25.

[96] U.S. Government Accountability Office, *Joint Strike Fighter[:] Additional Costs and Delays Risk Not Meeting Warfighter Requirements on Time*, GAO-10-382, March 2010.

[97] Ibid., pp. 42-45.

Testing Performance

During 2010, the F-35 had a mixed test record. DOD's annual report on F-35 testing indicated:

> The cumulative data for test sorties and points indicate progress slightly ahead of that planned. The test teams exceeded the goal of 394 total sorties for calendar year 2010 by early December 2010. However, progress in testing the Short Take-Off and Vertical Landing (STOVL) aircraft was less than planned... Immaturity of STOVL design and unexpected component deficiencies limited successful accomplishment of test points in areas critical to short take-off and vertical landing capability. Development of mission systems software continued to experience delays that affected flight test progress.[98]

"Overall, F-35 flight testing ended 2010 close to its goal of more than 3,700 test points, but while the CTOL F-35A and F-35C CV were well ahead of plan, Stovl and mission-system testing fell short. More than half the test points required for Stovl RFT and ship clearance remain to be accomplished in 2011."[99]

Robert Stevens, CEO of F-35 contractor Lockheed Martin, "said ... that several parts on the most complex version of its F-35 Joint Strike Fighter were failing more often than expected ... includ[ing] a fan that cools the engine and the hydraulic devices that open air-flow panels to provide the vertical thrust. He said valves, switches and power system components had also been unreliable."[100] As a consequence, "The U.S. may withhold from Lockheed as much as $614 million in fees because of delays on the warplane, pending improvements in flight tests, Defense Secretary Robert Gates has said."[101]

"Since March, F-35 BF-1, the only jet instrumented for vertical landings in the initial test phase, has accomplished about half as many vertical landings as scheduled, performing a dozen flights."[102] Also, "The short-takeoff-and-vertical-landing (Stovl) F-35B Joint Strike Fighter is unlikely to conduct initial at-sea testing on schedule in March 2011 because of delays in clearing the vertical-landing envelope ... [t]he delay could affect U.S. Marine Corps plans to declare initial operational capability (IOC) with the F-35B in late 2012."[103] "Originally set for March, ship trials are now slated between August and November."[104]

Although the F-35 program overall was running ahead of the test plan, with 427 test flights (against a plan of 390) by the end of 2010, the F-35B had flown only 216 of a planned 254 flights. As a result, "The US Marine Corps could declare initial operational capability with the Air Force's F-35A variant of the Joint Strike Fighter, as delays and a major review cast more doubt on the feasibility of meeting a late-2012 IOC date with the F-35B short take-off, vertical landing variant... Lockheed Martin F-35 general manager Tom Burbage said."[105] Further, "[w]hile the program exceeded its year-end target of 394 flights, the objectives of clearing the conventional-

[98] Director, Operational Test & Evaluation, *FY 2010 Annual Report*, December 2010, p. 13.

[99] Graham Warwick, "F-35 Begins Year With Test Objectives Unmet," *AviationWeek.com*, January 4, 2011.

[100] Christopher Drew, "Lockheed Says Several Parts For F-35s Are Failing," *The New York Times*, July 28, 2010.

[101] Tony Capaccio and Gopal Ratnam, "Lockheed F-35's Parts to Get More Scrutiny Amid Test Delays, Pentagon Says," *Bloomberg News*, August 3, 2010.

[102] Bill Sweetman, "Marines Could Fly CTOL JSF," *Aviation Week/Ares blog*, September 14, 2010.

[103] Graham Warwick, "STOVL F-35B To Miss Initial At-Sea Test Date," *Aerospace Daily*, September 17, 2010.

[104] Graham Warwick, "F-35 Begins Year With Test Objectives Unmet," *AviationWeek.com*, January 4, 2011.

[105] Sweetman, op. cit.

takeoff-and-landing (CTOL) variant to begin pilot training, and the short-takeoff-and-vertical-landing (Stovl) version for training and initial ship trials, were not accomplished as planned in 2010."[106]

The entire F-35 test fleet was grounded from October 1-5, 2010, to address fuel pump issues. To help regain schedule, the first two production aircraft have been retasked to flight test, although this will delay the start of Air Force flight training.[107]

2011 testing has gone much more to plan. The F-35C successfully completed jet-blast-deflector testing August 13.[108] The program expects to move two specially instrumented F-35Bs to the amphibious ship *Wasp* in the first week of October 2011. "This will kick off a series of shipboard tests to assess the interface between the stealthy, single-engine jet and the ship. During those trials, the test force plans to conduct 67 vertical landings on the ship.... Lockheed Martin officials say that despite a halt in test flights, they are 8% ahead of plans in year-to-date flights."[109]

Cost Tracking

On October 5, 2010, DOD decertified the system used by contractor Lockheed Martin to track the cost performance of the F-35 program.

> De-certification of the Fort Worth-based unit's "earned value management system" was intended to "help ensure Lockheed Martin devotes the needed attention to complete" corrective actions "in a timely manner," Pentagon spokeswoman Cheryl Irwin said in a statement via e-mail.[110]

Secretary Gates's January 2011 Program Restructure

The director of the F-35 program completed a baseline technical review of the program in late 2010, "which was a technical, 'bottoms-up,' independent review of the air vehicle platform, sustainment, mission systems software, and test."[111] Responding to issues detailed in the technical review, on January 6, 2011, Secretary of Defense Gates announced a change in the F-35 testing and production plan focused on the F-35B:

> In short, two of the JSF variants, the Air Force version and the Navy's carrier-based version, are proceeding satisfactorily.

> By comparison, the Marine Corps' short take-off and vertical-landing (STOVL) variant is experiencing significant testing problems. These issues may lead to a redesign of the aircraft's structure and propulsion, changes that could add yet more weight and more cost to an aircraft that has little capacity to absorb more of either.

---

[106] Graham Warwick, "F-35 Begins Year With Test Objectives Unmet," *AviationWeek.com*, January 4, 2011.

[107] "Test Reset," *Aerospace Daily*, November 8, 2010.

[108] *Defense Daily*, August 29, 2011.

[109] Amy Butler, "Lockheed Wraps Up F-35 Structural Testing," *AviationWeek.com*, September 20, 2011.

[110] "Lockheed Warned On Cost-Tracking," *The Washington Post*, October 6, 2010, p. 16.

[111] Director, Operational Test & Evaluation, *FY 2010 Annual Report*, December 2010, p. 13.

> As a result, I am placing the STOVL variant on the equivalent of a two-year probation. If we cannot fix this variant during this time frame and get it back on track in terms of performance, cost and schedule, then I believe it should be canceled.
>
> We will also move the development of the Marine variant to the back of the overall JSF production sequence.[112]

Three major technical issues emerged for the F-35B.

The first was premature wear on hinges for the auxiliary inlet door feeding the F-35B's lift fan, which caused the F-35B fleet to be grounded in September 2010. A technical fix was in place by January 2011.

Second, cracks were discovered in a bulkhead of an F-35B used for fatigue testing "after the airplane had been subjected to the equivalent of about 1,500 hours of flight time out of a total 16,000 hours planned." Prime contractor Lockheed Martin has redesigned the bulkhead, and "'(o)ther locations of similar design are also being assessed,' company spokesman John Kent said in an e-mailed statement Jan. 11."[113] The aluminum bulkhead is unique to the F-35B; "F-35A and F-35C bulkheads are still made of titanium, as are similar bulkheads on the F-22."[114]

Third, the driveshaft, lift-fan clutch, and actuator for the F-35B's roll-post nozzles will be redesigned following discovery that the driveshaft contracts and expands more than expected, and that the other components experience more heat than anticipated during flight operations.[115]

Moving F-35B development, which had been scheduled to lead the program, to the back of the queue should reduce the impact of F-35B issues on the schedule for the A and C models, which are encountering fewer development challenges.

The schedule changes Gates announced mean that "the Pentagon now plans to order 325 jets between 2012 and 2016, 124 fewer than anticipated a few months ago.... Of the money saved by buying fewer jets, $4.6 billion would pay for continued development and testing. Another $4 billion would be used by the Pentagon for other purposes, including acquiring more F/A-18 Super Hornets, one of the planes the F-35 is supposed to replace, for the Navy."[116] The F/A-18 buy is reportedly 41 aircraft.[117]

While there are no specific criteria for the F-35B to meet in order to exit probation, "program officials have begun restructuring the program to hit four key goals ... maintaining propulsion levels while reducing aircraft weight, ensuring the aircraft's ability to gain full flight clearance,

---

[112] Office of the Assistant Secretary of Defense (Public Affairs), "DOD News Briefing with Secretary Gates and Adm. Mullen from the Pentagon," press release, January 6, 2011, http://www.defense.gov/transcripts/transcript.aspx?transcriptid=4747.

[113] Dave Majumdar, "Lockheed: One F-35B Problem Fixed," *DefenseNews.com*, January 10, 2011.

[114] Bill Sweetman, "Major F-35B Component Cracks In Fatigue Test," *AviationWeek/Ares blog*, November 17, 2010.

[115] Stephen Trimble, "New design changes raises pressure on future of F-35B variant," *Flight International*, January 12, 2011.

[116] Bob Cox, "Defense Secretary Proposes Cutting 124 F-35 Purchases," *Fort Wiorth Star-Telegram*, January 7, 2011.

[117] Andrea Shalal-Esa, "Pentagon delays F-35, buys more Boeing fighters," *Reuters*, January 6, 2011.

proving the fighter's suitability for ship operations and hitting the program's key performance parameters."[118]

Fleet Grounding

All F-35s were grounded for approximately a week in March 2011, after the discovery of issues with onboard electrical generators. After discovering that improper maintenance, rather than a hardware issue, led to the problem, the fleet was returned to operation.[119]

Affordability and Projected Fighter Shortfalls

An additional potential issue for Congress for the F-35 program concerns the affordability of the F-35, particularly in the context of projected shortfalls in both Air Force fighters and Navy and Marine Corps strike fighters.

Although the F-35 was conceived as a relatively affordable strike fighter, some observers are concerned that in a situation of constrained DOD resources, F-35s might not be affordable in the annual quantities planned by DOD, at least not without reducing funding for other DOD programs. As the annual production rate of the F-35 increases, the program will require more than $10 billion per year in acquisition funding at the same time that DOD will face other budgetary challenges. The issue of F-35 affordability is part of a larger and long-standing issue concerning the overall affordability of DOD's tactical aircraft modernization effort, which also includes procurement of F/A-18E/Fs (through FY2012, at least).[120] Some observers who are concerned about the affordability of DOD's desired numbers of F-35s have suggested procuring upgraded F-16s as complements or substitutes for F-35As for the Air Force, and F/A-18E/Fs as complements or substitutes for F-35Cs for the Navy.[121] F-35 supporters argue that F-16s and F/A-18E/Fs are less capable than the F-35, and that the F-35 is designed to have reduced life-cycle costs.

The issue of F-35 affordability occurs in the context of a projected shortfall of up to 800 Air Force fighters that was mentioned by Air Force officials in 2008,[122] and a projected shortfall of more than 100 (and perhaps more than 200) Navy and Marine Corps strike fighters.[123] In the interim, "in light of delays with the F-35 Lightning II Joint Strike Fighter, the U.S. Air Force is set to begin looking at which of its newer F-16s will receive structural refurbishments, avionics updates, sensor upgrades or all three."[124]

---

[118] Carlo Munoz, "Venlet: No 'Black And White' Metrics To Evaluate Future of Suspended STOVL Program," *Defense Daily*, February 16, 2011.

[119] Dave Majumdar, "Maintenance Procedure Led to F-35 Generator Failure," *Defense News.com*, March 26, 2011.

[120] For more on this issue, see CRS Report RL33543, *Tactical Aircraft Modernization: Issues for Congress.*

[121] See, inter alia, George Wilson, "Kill the F-35?" *CongressDaily AM*, March 22, 2010.

[122] Testimony of Lieutenant General Daniel Darnell, Deputy Chief of Staff, Air, Space and Information Operations, Plans and Requirements, before an April 9, 2008, hearing on Air Force and Navy aviation programs before the Airland subcommittee of the Senate Armed Services Committee. (Source: Transcript of hearing.)

[123] For more on the projected Navy-Marine Corps strike fighter shortfall, see CRS Report RL30624, *Navy F/A-18E/F and EA-18G Aircraft Program.*

[124] John Reed, "JSF Woes Push AF to F-16s," *DoD Buzz*, November 4, 2010.

Future of Marine Corps Aviation

Britain's decision to withdraw from purchasing the F-35B leaves the U.S. Marine Corps as the only customer for that variant. The possibility of increasing unit cost due to lower quantities, coupled with the testing and development challenges unique to the STOVL B model, have led some commentators[125] to question whether the Marine Corps will or should continue to acquire the F-35B. Marine Corps doctrine states that the Marine Air Ground Task Force (MAGTF) must include organic tactical aviation assets. Some note that advances in threat make forward operation of STOVL aircraft increasingly impractical, and that Navy or Marine F-35Cs flown from carriers could provide air capability for forces ashore, as the British have chosen to do. Although conscious of the threat to forward operating bases, Under Secretary of the Navy Robert Work

> said that the Marine Corps' short take-off vertical-landing version of the Joint Strike Fighter, which has faced the most troubles in the turbulent JSF program, will still provide a vital capability.... "Having the flexibility of a short take-off vertical-landing aircraft that's supersonic, that's stealthy, that works in tandem with longer-range Navy systems off a wide variety of ships really provides us with a lot of capability," Work said.[126]

Implications for Industrial Base

Another potential issue for Congress regarding the F-35 program concerns its potential impact on the U.S. tactical aircraft industrial base. The award of the F-35 SDD contract to a single company (Lockheed Martin) raised concerns in Congress and elsewhere that excluding Boeing from this program would reduce that company's ability to continue designing and manufacturing fighter aircraft.[127]

Similar concerns regarding engine-making firms have been raised since 2006, when DOD first proposed (as part of the FY2007 budget submission) terminating the F136 alternate engine program. Some observers are concerned that that if the F136 were cancelled, General Electric would not have enough business designing and manufacturing fighter jet engines to continue competing in the future with Pratt and Whitney (the manufacturer of the F135 engine). Others argued that General Electric's considerable business in both commercial and military engines was sufficient to sustain General Electric's ability to produce this class of engine in the future.

Exports of the F-35 could also have a strong impact on the U.S. tactical aircraft industrial base through export. Most observers believe that the F-35 could potentially dominate the combat aircraft export market, much as the F-16 has. Like the F-16, the F-35 appears to be attractive because of its relatively low cost, flexible design, and promise of high performance. Competing fighters and strike fighters, including France's Rafale, Sweden's JAS Gripen, and the Eurofighter Typhoon, are positioned to challenge the F-35 in the fighter export market.

Some observers are concerned that by allowing foreign companies to participate in the F-35 program, DOD may be inadvertently opening up U.S. markets to foreign competitors who enjoy

---

[125] See, *inter alia,* Bill Sweetman, "The Next JSF Debate," *Aviation Week/Ares blog*, October 25, 2010.

[126] Cid Standifer, "Joint Amphibious Assaults Will Be Phased, Count On Air Force And Army," *Inside the Navy*, August 9, 2010.

[127] For more information, see CRS Report RL31360, *Joint Strike Fighter (JSF): Potential National Security Questions Pertaining to a Single Production Line*, by Christopher Bolkcom and Daniel H. Else.

direct government subsidies. A May 2004 GAO report found that the F-35 program could "significantly impact" the U.S. and global industrial base.[128] GAO found that two laws designed to protect segments of the U.S. defense industry—the Buy American Act and the Preference for Domestic Specialty Metals clause—would have no impact on decisions regarding which foreign companies would participate in the F-35 program, because DOD has decided that foreign companies that participate in the F-35 program, and which have signed reciprocal procurement agreements with DOD to promote defense cooperation, are eligible for a waiver.

Legislative Activity for FY2012

Summary of Quantities and Funding

Table 4 summarizes congressional action on F-35 FY2011 procurement quantities and procurement and research and development funding levels.

Table 4. Summary of Action on FY2012 F-35 Quantities and Funding

Funding figures in millions of dollars, rounded to nearest tenth

	Request	Authorization (H.R. 1540/S. 1253)			Appropriations (S. 3800/H.R. 2219)		
		HASC report	SASC report	Conference report	HAC report	SAC report	Conference report
Procurement quantities							
F-35As (Air Force)	19	19	19	18	19	17	18
F-35Bs (Marine Corps)	6	6	6	6	6	6	6
F-35Cs (Navy)	7	7	7	7	7	6	7
Total	32	32	32	31	32	29	31
Procurement funding							
Air Force procurement funding	3,340.6	3,340.6	3,340.6	3,189.6a	3,340.6	3,038.6	3,289.6a
Air Force advance procurement funding	323.5	323.5	323.5	229.0	323.5	229.0	229.0
Navy procurement funding	2,645.0b	2,645.0	2,645.0	2,590.0	2,590.0c	2,455.0	2,590.0

---

[128] General Accountability Office, *Joint Strike Fighter Acquisition: Observations on the Supplier Base*, GAO-04-554, May 2004.

Navy advance procurement funding	334.9[d]	334.9	334.9	226.3	334.9	226.3	226.3
Research and development funding							
Air Force	1,435.7[e]	1,435.7	1,435.7	1,397.8[f]	1,397.8[g]	1,387.9[g]	1,387.9
Navy	1,348.2[h]	1,348.2	1,348.2	1,276.3	1,276.3[i]	1,276.3[i]	1,276.3

Source: Prepared by CRS based on committee reports, bill text, and floor amendments.

a. $151 million cut for 1 aircraft; $100 million added (from initial spares execution) to cover concurrency costs.

b. $1,503.1 million for 7 F-35Cs; 1,141.9 million for 6 F-35Bs.

c. $1,448.1 million for 7 F-35Cs, $1,141.9 million for 6 F-35Bs. The HAC cut $20.0 million for engineering change order carryover, $30 million for peculiar ground support equipment growth, and $5 million for logistic (sic) support growth.

d. $217.7 million for F-35C; $117.2 million for F-35B.

e. $1,387.9M for JSF EMD and $47.8M for F-35 Squadrons.

f. Authorizers cut $37.9 million from F-35 Squadrons for Block IV software development ahead of need.

g. The HAC cut $37.9 million from JSF EMD and the SAC $47.8 million from F-35 Squadrons for Block IV software development ahead of need.

h. $650.8 million Navy; $670.7 million Marine Corps; $26.7 million United States Research Laboratory (sensor upgrades)

i. The authorization conference, HAC, and SAC all cut $37.9 million ($18.937M each from the Navy and Marine Corps) for Block IV software development ahead of need.

FY2012 Defense Authorization Act (H.R. 1540/S. 1253)

House

As passed by the House, H.R. 1540 included two significant provisions relating to the F-35. Both concerned the F-35 alternate engine program, and as such are covered in greater detail in CRS Report R41131, *F-35 Alternate Engine Program: Background and Issues for Congress*. They are:

SECTION 215—LIMITATION ON OBLIGATION OF FUNDS FOR THE PROPULSION SYSTEM FOR THE F-35 LIGHTNING II AIRCRAFT PROGRAM

This section would limit the obligation or expenditure of funds for performance improvements to the F-35 Lightning II propulsion system unless the Secretary of Defense ensures the competitive development and production of such propulsion system. This section would define the term `performance improvement,' with respect to the propulsion system for the F-35 Lightning II aircraft program, as an increase in fan or core engine airflow volume or maximum thrust in military or afterburner setting for the primary purpose of improving the take-off performance or vertical load bring back of such aircraft, and would not include development or procurement improvements with respect to weight, acquisition cost, operations and support costs, durability, manufacturing efficiencies, observability requirements, or repair costs.

SECTION 252—PRESERVATION AND STORAGE OF CERTAIN PROPERTY RELATED TO F136 PROPULSION SYSTEM

This section would require the Secretary of Defense to develop and carry out a plan for the preservation and storage of property owned by the Federal Government that was acquired under the F136 propulsion system development contract that would: ensure that the Secretary preserves and stores such property in a manner that would allow the development of the F136 propulsion system to be restarted after a period of idleness, provide for the long-term sustainment and repair of such property, and allow for such preservation and storage to be conducted at either the facilities of the Federal Government or a contractor under such contract; identify supplier base costs of restarting development; ensure that the Secretary, at no cost to the Federal Government, provides support and allows for the use of such property by the contractor under such contract to conduct research, development, test, and evaluation of the F136 engine, if such activities are self-funded by the contractor; and identify any contract modifications, additional facilities or funding that the Secretary determines necessary to carry out the plan. This section would also prohibit the obligation or expenditure of amounts authorized to be appropriated by this Act or otherwise make available for fiscal year 2012 for research, development, test, and evaluation, Navy, or research, development, test and evaluation, Air Force, for the F-35 Lightning II program for activities related to destroying or disposing of the property acquired under the F136 propulsion system development contract. Additionally, this section would require the Secretary of Defense to submit a report to the congressional defense committee, not later than 45 days after the enactment of the Act, on the Secretary's plan for the preservation and storage of such property.

H.Rept. 112-78, accompanying H.R. 1540, discussed these provisions and one other recommended change to the F-35 program:

F-35 aircraft

The budget request contained $2.7 billion in PEs 64800F, 64800N, and 64800M for development of the F-35 aircraft, but contained no funds for development of a competitive F-35 propulsion system. The F-35 is also known as the Joint Strike Fighter (JSF).

The competitive F-35 propulsion system program has been developing the F136 engine, which would have provided a competitive alternative to the currently-planned F135 engine. For the past 5 years, the committee recommended increases for the F-35 competitive propulsion system, and notes funds have been appropriated by Congress for this purpose through the first half of fiscal year 2011. Despite section 213 of the National Defense Authorization Act for Fiscal Year 2008 (P.L. 110-181), which required the Secretary of Defense to obligate and expend sufficient annual amounts for the continued development and procurement of a competitive propulsion system for the F-35, the committee is disappointed that the Department of Defense (DOD) has, for the sixth consecutive year, chosen not to comply with both the spirit and intent of this law, by opting not to include funds for this purpose in the budget request. According to the Department of Defense, the life-cycle cost of the F-35 engine program is $110.0 billion. A January 10, 2011, report by the Congressional Research Service notes that there has never been a separate engine competition for F-35 engines. The committee notes that the Department of Defense terminated the F136 contract on April 25, 2011.

On February 23, 2010, the Deputy Secretary of Defense submitted to the committee an update of the 2007 Department of Defense report, `Joint Strike Fighter Alternate Engine Acquisition and Independent Cost Analysis' for the competitive engine program, which noted that an investment of $2.9 billion over 6 years in additional cost would be required to finish F136 engine development and to conduct directed buys to prepare the F136 for competitive procurement of F-35 engines in 2017. This report also projected that long-term costs for either a one-engine or two-engine competitive acquisition strategy would be the same, on a net present value basis. Last September, the Government Accountability Office

(GAO) reported that this estimate was based on two key assumptions made by the Department of Defense in developing the $2.9 billion funding projection that have significant impact on the estimated amount of upfront investment needed. These assumptions were: (1) four years of noncompetitive procurements of both engines would be needed to allow the alternate engine contractor sufficient time to gain production experience and complete developmental qualification of the engine, and (2) the Government would need to fund quality and reliability improvements for engine components. GAO notes that past studies and historical data it examined indicate that it may take less than 4 years of noncompetitive procurements and that competition may obviate the need for the Government to fund component improvement programs. GAO concludes that if these conditions hold true for the alternate engine, the funding projection for the alternate engine could be lower than DOD's projection.

The committee notes that reports on the F-35 alternate engine program completed in 2007 by the Institute for Defense Analyses, GAO, and the Department of Defense all agree that non-financial benefits of a competitive engine program include improved contractor responsiveness, a more robust industrial base, improved operational readiness, better engine performance, and technological innovation. The committee further notes that the 2007 study by the Institute for Defense Analyses on the JSF engine cost analysis noted that, `In 2035, the JSF would comprise 95 percent of the fighter attack force structure.' Among other reasons, the committee remains concerned about proceeding with a $110.0 billion, sole-source engine program for that percentage of the Department of Defense's future tactical fighter fleets.

The committee is also concerned about the operational risk of having a one engine program for the F-35 fleet, and notes that a former F-35 Program Executive Officer has stated, `The Pentagon needs to carefully consider the operational risk of having just one engine for the F-35 fighter jet. Competition could bring faster technology development and lower costs. A single engine could be worrisome if an engine problem ever grounded the fighters. In the past, having a variety of fighters meant the Pentagon could use other planes to offset any groundings, like an 11-month engine-related halt in Harriers in 2000. I simply think that we've focused too much on the discussion about cost benefit and not the operational risk benefit.'

The committee also notes that section 3, titled `Scope of Work', of the 2006 memorandum of understanding (MOU) signed by all JSF partner nation senior defense officials regarding the production, sustainment, and follow-on development of the Joint Strike Fighter states that `the production work will include, but will not be limited to, the following: Production of the JSF air vehicle, including propulsion systems, both F135 and F136.' The committee understands that this MOU is still current.

The committee further notes that, `The Final Report of the Quadrennial Defense Review Independent Panel' published on July 29, 2010, states: `History has shown that the only reliable source of price reduction through the life of a program is competition between dual sources.' Consistent with that view, the committee strongly supports the December 2010 announcement by the Department of Defense that the Littoral Combat Ship (LCS) program would award a contract to 2 contractors for 10 ships each. The budget request contained $1.9 billion through fiscal year 2016 for continued LCS development. Like the LCS program, the F-35 competitive engine program would also require development funding in the Future Years Defense Program, and the committee is perplexed why the Department would implement a dual-source acquisition strategy for the LCS program and not for the F-35 competitive engine program.

The committee believes that the F-35 competitive engine program has its roots in the F-16 alternate engine program which began in the early 1980s. Often called, `The Great Engine

War' the committee notes that Robert Drewes, in his 1987 book, `The Air Force and The Great Engine War,' wrote: `Competition is the only sure way to get the best effort. Competition did yield ... some substantial initial benefits to the Air Force ... engine improvements [were offered] to the Air Force earlier than the Air Force had been led to expect without the competition. Furthermore, unit prices were lower than ... had previously been offer[ed]. Since the initial split buy in February 1984, competition further induced [the contractor] to grant even more concessions to the Air Force. Warranty prices have been reduced significantly and arrangements with the European Participating Governments have improved.'

The committee believes it is too early to have terminated the F136 development contract because it was 2 years after initial operational capability for the F-15 that problems first became apparent with the F-15 and F-16 F100 engine that resulted in the first alternate engine program, an equivalent point in time for the F-35, 7 years from now. The F-35 primary engine has 1,000 flight hours. The Department of Defense standard to achieve maturity on an engine requires 200,000 flight hours. In response to section 211 of the John Warner National Defense Authorization Act for Fiscal Year 2007 (P.L. 109-364), on March 15, 2007, the GAO presented to the committee, `Analysis of Costs for the Joint Strike Fighter Program,' which stated that experience suggests that competition between the F135 and F136 can generate savings and benefits up to 20 percent if:

(1) Contractors are incentivized to achieve more aggressive production learning curves;

(2) Annual completion for procurement is kept in place over an extended period;

(3) Contractors produce more reliable engine, resulting in lower maintenance costs; and

(4) Contractors invest additional corporate money to remain competitive.

For these reasons, the committee remains steadfast in its belief that continuing the F-35 competitive propulsion system program would be the right course of action for the F-35 propulsion system.

The committee understands that the F136 contractor intends to provide its own funds to continue F136 development for fiscal year 2012. Accordingly, elsewhere in this title, the committee includes a provision that would preserve and store property related to the F136 contract, and would ensure that the Secretary of Defense, at no cost to the Federal Government, provides support and allows for the use of such property by the contractor under a contract to conduct research, development, test, and evaluation of the F136 engine, if such activities are self-funded by the contractor.

F-35 alternative ejection seat

The budget request contained $11.2 million in PE 64706F for Life Support Systems. Of this amount, no funding was requested for an F-35A alternative ejection seat.

The committee notes that the Department of the Air Force has benefited from a common family of ejection seats in its tactical aircraft fleet since the late 1970s. The committee understands that preliminary internal Air Force studies have determined that the potential exists for significant cost savings and increased pilot safety with an alternative ejection seat system for the F-35A. The committee also notes that the Department of Commerce has expressed concern about risks to national security if the United States becomes totally reliant on foreign sources for ejection seat technology. Accordingly, the committee believes the Department of Defense should be particularly mindful of these issues in evaluating competitive options for F-35A ejection seat program.

The committee understands that the Department of the Air Force is conducting a business-case analysis to determine whether an alternative F-35A ejection seat offers substantial F-35A life-cycle cost savings and commonality benefits to the Department of the Air Force tactical fighter fleets, while also considering the impacts on the Department of the Navy F-35B and F-35C programs as well as the F-35 program's international partners. The committee believes that the F-35 program's ejection seat requirement should be reviewed in the context of this analysis. If a decision to change the F-35A's ejection seat requirement is warranted by the business-case analysis, the committee urges the qualification and integration of an alternative ejection seat in the F-35A.

The committee recommends $11.2 million in PE 64706F for Life Support Systems.

Senate

The Senate Armed Services Committee-reported version of S. 1253 included language on two F-35 issues:

SEC. 152. F-35 JOINT STRIKE FIGHTER AIRCRAFT.

In entering into a contract for the procurement of aircraft for the fifth low-rate initial production contract lot (LRIP-5) for the F-35 Lightning II Joint Strike Fighter aircraft, the Secretary of Defense shall ensure each of the following:

(1) That the contract is a fixed price contract.

(2) That the contract requires the contractor to assume full responsibility for costs under the contract above the target cost specified in the contract.

SEC. 153. REPORT ON PLAN TO IMPLEMENT WEAPON SYSTEMS ACQUISITION REFORM ACT OF 2009 MEASURES WITHIN THE JOINT STRIKE FIGHTER AIRCRAFT PROGRAM.

At the same time the budget of the President for fiscal year 2013 is submitted to Congress pursuant to section 1105 of title 31, United States Code, the Under Secretary for Acquisition, Technology, and Logistics shall submit to the Committees on Armed Services of the Senate and the House of Representatives a report on the plans of the Department of Defense to implement the requirements of the Weapon Systems Acquisition Reform Act of 2009 (P.L. 111-23), and the amendments made by that Act, within the Joint Strike Fighter (JSF) aircraft program. The report shall set forth the following:

(1) Specific goals for implementing the requirements of the Weapon Systems Acquisition Reform Act of 2009, and the amendments made by that Act, within the Joint Strike Fighter aircraft program.

(2) A schedule for achieving each goal set forth under paragraph (1) for the Joint Strike Fighter aircraft program.

The accompanying SASC report (S.Rept. 112-26, accompanying S. 1253) expanded on those items:[129]

---

[129] The SASC report also included a significant additional view by Senator John McCain regarding oversight of the F-35 program, which can be found on pages 316-317 of the report.

F-35 Joint Strike Fighter Aircraft (sec. 152)

The committee recommends a provision that would require the Secretary of Defense to ensure that, in entering into a contract for the fifth low-rate initial production (LRIP) contract lot for the F-35 Lightning II Joint Strike Fighter (JSF) aircraft: (1) the contract is a fixed price contract; and (2) the contract requires the contractor to assume full responsibility for costs under the contract above the target cost specified in the contract.

The Department has made the JSF program the cornerstone of its tactical aviation modernization strategy. Because of its critical contribution to future force capability, the committee supports continued development and acquisition of the JSF, but not at any cost. This provision supports getting the program on track and keeping it there.

By requiring the contractor to assume full responsibility for all costs under the contract above the target cost level, the committee is reflecting its grave concern that LRIP-4 contract allows the contractor to be awarded a considerable fee even in the event of significant cost growth under that contract. The committee will be monitoring the program's performance under the LRIP-4 contract very closely.

The committee appreciates that there may be constructive changes to the LRIP-5 contract that the Defense Department may need to negotiate, based on changes that derive from the continuing system development and demonstration program, or from other valid government requirements. Those constructive changes may cause an increase in cost relative to the target cost, which should be borne by the government.

Report on plan to implement Weapon Systems Acquisition Reform Act of 2009 measures within the Joint Strike Fighter aircraft program (sec. 153)

The committee recommends a provision that would require the Under Secretary of Defense for Acquisition, Technology, and Logistics to produce a report on the Under Secretary's plans for implementing provisions of the Weapon Systems Acquisition Reform Act of 2009 (P.L. 111-23) for the F-35 Joint Strike Fighter (JSF) program. The provision would require that the Under Secretary submit that report at the same time as the President submits his budget request for fiscal year 2013.

The statement of managers accompanying the National Defense Authorization Act for Fiscal Year 2010 (P.L. 111-84) discussed potential competition of life support systems for the JSF program. Section 202 of the Weapon Systems Acquisition Reform Act of 2009 requires that the Secretary of Defense ensure that the acquisition strategy of every major defense acquisition program (MDAP) includes `measures to ensure competition, or the option of competition, at both the prime contract level and the subcontract level (at such tier or tiers as are appropriate) of such program throughout the life-cycle of such program as a means to improve contractor performance....' The Act also lists a number of measures that such competition may include if such measures are cost-effective. These measures include dual sourcing and unbundling of contracts.

The statement of managers also said, `As the Defense Department's largest MDAP, the conferees believe the F-35 program should be one of the first to benefit from implementation of the Weapon Systems Acquisition Reform Act of 2009. The conferees expect that, over the next budget cycle, the Department and the F-35 Program Executive Office (PEO) will develop a specific plan for how the F-35 PEO will implement the provisions of that Act.'

As far as the committee has been able to determine, the Department has taken no action on developing such a strategic plan for the JSF program. The committee understands that the program has been in turmoil for the past 2 years. However, with overall program cost control a major concern, and recent testimony by the Under Secretary that projected life cycle costs of the JSF are unaffordable, the committee believes that action to implement the Act for the JSF program is long overdue.

Final Action

The conference report accompanying H.R. 1540 as passed included the following text:

SEC. 143. F–35 JOINT STRIKE FIGHTER AIRCRAFT.

In entering into a contract for the procurement of aircraft for the sixth and all subsequent low-rate initial production contract lots for the F–35 Lightning II Joint Strike Fighter aircraft, the Secretary of Defense shall ensure each of the following:

(1) That the contract is a fixed-price contract.

(2) That the contract requires the contractor to assume full responsibility for costs under the contract above the target cost specified in the contract.

SEC. 148. REPORT ON PROBATIONARY PERIOD IN DEVELOPMENT OF SHORT TAKE-OFF, VERTICAL LANDING VARIANT OF THE JOINT STRIKE FIGHTER.

Not later than 45 days after the date of the enactment of this Act, the Secretary of Defense shall submit to the congressional defense committees a report on the development of the short take-off, vertical landing variant of the Joint Strike Fighter (otherwise known as the F–35B Joint Strike Fighter) that includes the following:

(1) An identification of the criteria that the Secretary determines must be satisfied before the F–35B Joint Strike Fighter can be removed from the two-year probationary status imposed by the Secretary on or about January 6, 2011.

(2) A mid-probationary period assessment of—

(A) the performance of the F–35B Joint Strike Fighter based on the criteria described in paragraph (1); and (B) the technical issues that remain in the development program for the F–35B Joint Strike Fighter.

(3) A plan for how the Secretary intends to resolve the issues described in paragraph (2)(B) before January 6, 2013.

SEC. 215. LIMITATION ON OBLIGATION OF FUNDS FOR THE F–35 LIGHTNING II AIRCRAFT PROGRAM.

Of the funds authorized to be appropriated by this Act or otherwise made available for fiscal year 2012 for research and development for the F–35 Lightning II aircraft program, not more that 80 percent may be obligated or expended until the date on which the Secretary of Defense certifies to the congressional defense committees that the acquisition strategy for the F–35 Lightning II aircraft includes a plan for achieving competition throughout operation and sustainment, in accordance with section 202(d) of the Weapon Systems Acquisition Reform Act of 2009 (Public Law 111–23; 10 U.S.C. 2430 note).

SEC. 223. PRESERVATION AND STORAGE OF CERTAIN PROPERTY RELATED TO F136 PROPULSION SYSTEM.

(a) PLAN.—The Secretary of Defense shall develop a plan for the disposition of property owned by the Federal Government that was acquired under the F136 propulsion system development contract.

The plan shall—

(1) ensure that the Secretary preserves and stores, uses, or disposes of such property in a manner that—

(A) provides for the long-term sustainment and repair of such property pending the determination by the Department of Defense that such property—

(i) can be used within the F–35 Lightning II aircraft program, in other Government development programs, or in other contractor-funded development activities;

(ii) can be stored for use in future Government development programs; or

(iii) should be disposed; and

(B) allows for such preservation and storage of identified property to be conducted at either the facilities of the Federal Government or a contractor under such contract; and

(2) identify any contract modifications, additional facilities, or funding that the Secretary determines necessary to carry out the plan.

(b) RESTRICTION ON THE USE OF FUNDS.—None of the amounts authorized to be appropriated by this Act or otherwise made available for fiscal year 2012 for research, development, test, and evaluation, Navy, or research, development, test, and evaluation, Air Force, for the F–35 Lightning II aircraft program may be obligated or expended for activities related to destroying or disposing of the property described in subsection (a) until the date that is 30 days after the date on which the report under subsection (c) is submitted to the congressional defense committees.

(c) REPORT.—Not later than 120 days after the date of the enactment of this Act, the Secretary of Defense shall submit to the congressional defense committees a report on the plan under subsection (a). That report shall describe how the Secretary intends to obtain maximum benefit to the Federal Government from the investment already made in developing the F136.

FY2012 Defense Appropriations Act (H.R. 2219/S. TBD)

House

The House Appropriations Committee report (H.Rept. 112-110, accompanying H.R. 2219) stated:

JOINT STRIKE FIGHTER

The Committee remains committed to the success of the F-35 Joint Strike Fighter (JSF) program. The recommendation provides funding for the procurement of 32 JSF aircraft, the same as the President's request. Additionally, with the exception of $75,748,000 for the premature development of the Block IV mission system software, the recommendation provides funding at the requested level for the continuation of the development effort for the aircraft.

The Committee understands the importance of this program to the future of the Nation's tactical aircraft inventory and our future national security. The F-35 will provide the United States and our allies the advanced sensor, precision strike, firepower, and stealth capabilities that are required well into the future.

The F-35B variant, which will be flown by the Marine Corps, has shown a very positive trend in flight testing thus far in fiscal year 2011 relative to its accomplishments in fiscal year 2010. Accordingly, the Committee encourages the Secretary of Defense to continue to closely monitor the progress of the F-35B test program and increase the production of the F-35B variant if the positive trend continues.

The Committee will continue to provide strong support and oversight for the JSF program and is committed to working with the Secretary of Defense to ensure the success of this program.

Senate

The Senate Appropriations Committee report (S.Rept. 112-77, accompanying H.R. 2219) stated:

> *Joint Strike Fighter-* The Committee fully supports the Joint Strike Fighter program and is encouraged by progress made in the testing program and improved delivery rates of aircraft. However, the Committee notes this recent progress occurred only after implementation of stern programmatic and contractual adjustments directed by the Secretary of Defense. The Committee remains concerned with the severe concurrency of development testing and production, noting that as production rates are increasing, the program has only completed 10 percent of its development testing.
>
> The F-22 aircraft experienced similar concurrency. The configuration of the first few lots of production aircraft differed from later aircraft. To ensure affordability of future modification, sustainment, and operations of the F-22 fleet, the Air Force upgraded the configuration of 81 F-22 aircraft at a total cost of $700,000,000. In addition to this cost, the Air Force has spent or plans to spend an additional $9,400,000,000 on continued F-22 modernization. Given current production projections of the Joint Strike Fighter, the Department will have contracted for 167 aircraft prior to full qualification of the aircraft hardware. Moreover, this quantity could increase to 229 aircraft if the full qualification efforts continue at the current pace. Based on F-22 experience, a common configuration modification for the Joint Strike Fighter program would cost approximately $10,000,000 per aircraft resulting in a $1,670,000,000 to $2,290,000,000 modification program. This cost is in addition to concurrency and performance cost growth of which the program is already projecting $771,200,000 for the first three lots of aircraft.
>
> The Department and the Joint Strike Fighter prime contractor have argued that increased production rates are necessary to reduce per unit cost due to the large amount of fixed costs on the program. However, the advertised per unit cost does not include additional costs to the program associated with performance, concurrency, and common configuration modifications. Similar performance, concurrency, and common configuration issues cost an additional $56,000,000 per aircraft on the F-22 program, none of which were ever accounted for in the per unit cost. If the Joint Strike Fighter continues on the same path and its costs are not brought under control, the Committee believes that the program's future could be in jeopardy.

Therefore, in order to begin reigning in future costs and to help keep the Joint Strike Fighter program affordable, the Committee recommends holding the total near-term production quantities at fiscal year 2011 levels to allow time to complete full hardware qualification of the Joint Strike Fighter aircraft. As such, the Committee recommends a reduction of Conventional Take-off and Landing aircraft procurement by two aircraft and advance procurement by seven aircraft, and the Carrier Variant procurement by one aircraft and advance procurement by six aircraft.

Final Action

As detailed in the Joint Explanatory Statement of the Committee of Conference, H.R. 2055 reduced the requested funding for the F-35 by $151 million in Aircraft Procurement, Air Force for one F-35A and by $94.5 million for advance procurement of F-35As. $100 million was added for "concurrency costs." Aircraft Procurement, Navy funds were reduced by $109 million from the budget request for advance procurement of F-35Cs. This left F-35 procurement funding at $5.9 billion for 31 aircraft, plus $455 million in advance procurement.

$37.874 million was cut from the request for Research and Development, Air Force under F-35 Squadrons as "Block 4 development early to need." Research and Development, Navy funding was reduced by $38 million for "Block IV development early to need."

Text included in the Joint Explanatory Statement stated:

> JOINT STRIKE FIGHTER
>
> The conference agreement reduces the budget request by $151,000,000 for the procurement of one F-35A Conventional Take-off and Landing aircraft, by $94,500,000 for advance procurement of Conventional Take-off and Landing aircraft, and by $109,000,000 for advance procurement of Carrier Variant aircraft. Additionally, the conferees are concerned with the cost of concurrency changes on the Joint Strike Fighter program and provide $100,000,000 to help offset the cost of concurrency for lot six aircraft and previously procured aircraft. The conferees encourage the Joint Strike Fighter Team to review processes and oversight of concurrency changes and establish a process that will reduce the time it takes to discover a problem, develop a solution, and implement this solution to reduce future concurrency change costs.
>
> The conferees recognize that, for a variety of reasons, the Joint Strike Fighter program is burdened with what could be the highest level of concurrency ever seen in an acquisition program. Therefore, the conferees direct the Secretary of Defense to provide a semi-annual report to the congressional defense committees that shows the actual.concurrency costs for the Joint Strike Fighter program. The report showing these actual concurrency costs shall be made available to the Director, Cost Assessment and Program Evaluation for the purposes of cost estimating and to develop lessons learned from allowing programmatic concurrency, so this cost can be considered when decisions are made regarding allowing such a high degree of concurrency in future programs.

Appendix A. Legislative Activity for FY2011

Summary of Quantities and Funding

Table A-1 summarizes congressional action on F-35 FY2011 procurement quantities and procurement and research and development funding levels.

Table A-1. Summary of Action on FY2011 F-35 Quantities and Funding

(Funding figures in millions of dollars, rounded to nearest tenth)

		Authorization (H.R. 6523/S. 3454)			Appropriations (S. 3800/H.R. 1473)		
	Request	HASC report	SASC report	Conference report (did not include program-level funding numbers)	HAC report	SAC report	Conference report
Procurement quantities							
F-35As (Air Force)	23[a]	22[b]	22[b]	N/A	N/A	16[b]	25
F-35Bs (Marine Corps)	13	13	13	N/A	N/A	10	3
F-35Cs (Navy)	7	7	7	N/A	N/A	6	7
Total	43	42	42	N/A	N/A	32	35
Procurement funding							
Air Force procurement funding	4,191.1[c]	3,986.2[b]	3.986.2[b]	N/A	N/A	3,028.7[bd]	4,064.4[e]
Air Force advance procurement funding	257.0	257.0	257.0	N/A	N/A	257.0	257.0
Navy procurement funding	4,243.1[f]	4,243.1	4,243.1	N/A	N/A	3,186.9[g]	2,208.8[h]
Navy advance procurement funding	219.9	219.9	219.9	N/A	N/A	219.9	219.9
Research and development funding							
Air Force	883.8	1,287.2[i]		N/A	N/A	1,051.2[k]	TBD
Navy	1,375.7	1,560.2[j]		N/A	N/A	1,267.7[l]	TBD

Source: Prepared by CRS based on committee reports, bill text, and floor amendments.

a. One F-35A was proposed to be funded from Overseas Contingency Operations (OCO) accounts.

b. All committee reports recommended deleting $204.0 million for the one OCO-funded aircraft.

c. $204.9 million of this amount was proposed to come from OCO accounts for one aircraft.

d. The SAC cut $730.2 million for 6 F-35As.

e. Cut $608.5M for 5 aircraft; added 974M transfer from F-35B; cut 60M for production support carryover; transferred $29.7M from F-35A modification line per AF request.

f. $1,667 million for F-35Cs; 2,576.1 million for F-35Bs.

g. The SAC cut $209.6 million for one F-35C, and $560.4 million for 3 F-35Bs.

h. $1.667 million for 7 F-35Cs, $555.7 million for 3 F-35Bs.

i. The HASC added $160.9 million transfer from F-35 squadron funds as requested by the Air Force, and $242.5 million for the F-35 alternate engine program.

j. The HASC cut $58.1 million for Block 4 software and added $242.6 million for the F-35 alternate engine program.

k. Includes $159.8 million transfer from F-35 squadron funds and $7.6 million transfer from Aircraft Procurement, Air Force for Auto GCAS (both requested by the Air Force).

l. The SAC cut $50.0 million for underexecution of the test program and $58.0 million to defer development of Block 4 software.

FY2011 Defense Authorization Act (H.R. 5136/S. 3454)

House

H.Rept. 111-491, accompanying H.R. 5136, recommended several changes to the F-35 program, including

SECTION 141—LIMITATION ON PROCUREMENT OF F-35 LIGHTNING II AIRCRAFT

This section would limit the obligation or expenditure of amounts necessary for the procurement of F-35 aircraft to an amount necessary for the procurement of 30 such aircraft unless the Under Secretary of Defense for Acquisition, Technology, and Logistics and the Director of Operational Test and Evaluation submit certifications to the congressional defense committees, not later than January 15, 2011, that specified items pertaining to the F-35 program have been accomplished. The section would also allow the Secretary of Defense to waive the full achievement of some items if the Under Secretary of Defense for Acquisition, Technology, and Logistics certifies that the failure to fully achieve some items would not delay or otherwise negatively affect the F-35 aircraft test schedule for FY2011, impede production of 42 F-35 aircraft in such fiscal year, and otherwise increase risk to the F-35 aircraft program.

Under Items of Special Interest in Aircraft Procurement, Air Force, the House report stated:

F-35 modifications

The budget request contained $94.2 million for F-35 modifications, of which $86.6 million was included to procure 25 kits to retrofit 25 low-rate initial production (LRIP) F-35A aircraft to the block three configuration.

Under the recently-revised F-35 schedule, the committee notes that development of block three hardware and software components will not be complete until 2015, and believes that the request to procure kits to retrofit 25 LRIP F-35A aircraft to the block three configuration is premature.

Accordingly, the committee recommends $7.6 million, a decrease of $86.6 million for F-35A modifications.

Senate

The SASC report's[130] main discussion of F-35 issues was included under Title XV, concerning Overseas Contingency Operations.

Joint Strike Fighter

The budget request included $1,887.0 million in Aircraft Procurement, Navy (APN), to purchase 7 Joint Strike Fighter (JSF) aircraft for the Navy (F–35C), $2,576.1 million in APN for 13 JSF aircraft for the Marine Corps (F–35B), and $3,986.2 million in Aircraft Procurement, Air Force (APAF) for 22 JSF for the Air Force (F–35A). In addition, the budget request for Overseas Contingency Operations (OCO) include $204.9 million in APAF for 1 F–35A to replace one legacy aircraft lost in combat operations.

Since last year, the Department found significant problems in the performance of the F–35 contractor team in conducting the elements of the system development and demonstration (SDD) phase of the program, which have led to delays in developmental testing of the aircraft. The Department restructured the program in conjunction with submitting the fiscal year 2011 budget by taking a number of actions, including: (1) extending the development test schedule to March 2015; (2) adding additional research, development, testing, and evaluation (RDT&E) funds to pay for mitigating known risks; (3) buying another carrier variant developmental test aircraft and add another software integration line to the program; (4) using up to three aircraft procured under low-rate initial production (LRIP) contracts for developmental testing; (5) reducing procurement quantities over the future-years defense program (FYDP) to slow the planned production ramp up in later years and offset added funding for developmental testing; and (6) installing a new fee structure that would provide incentives for the contractor team to achieve key performance events and cost goals.

Last year, Congress approved funding for 30 aircraft. This year, the budget request is for a total of 43 F–35 aircraft of all types. The number of 43 aircraft matches what had been the planned production rate for the F–35 aircraft 2 years ago before any of these problems and delays became evident. The FYDP for fiscal year 2009 included a plan to buy 43 JSF aircraft in 2011, although the mix of F–35A and F–35C aircraft changed by one aircraft each.

The committee understands that the Department would prefer to get JSF aircraft sooner. However, the fact that the production changes recommended by the Department in this restructuring only affect production plans later in the FYDP means that the concurrency in the program for fiscal year 2011 has actually increased.

The committee believes that a more modest ramp up in production to a total of 42 aircraft in the near-term would lessen that concurrency, while increasing the production rate from 30 aircraft to allow the program to demonstrate that the production processes and management systems will support growing to higher levels later in the FYDP.

Therefore, the committee recommends a reduction of $204.9 million in the APAF account within OCO.

---

[130] S.Rept. 111-201, accompanying S. 3454.

Also, Section 141 of the Senate report stated

System management plan and matrix for the F–35 Joint Strike Fighter Aircraft Program

The committee recommends a provision that would require that the Secretary of Defense establish a system management plan and matrix for the F–35 Joint Strike Fighter (JSF) program that would be used to measure progress in gaining maturity for the system during the remainder of the system development and demonstration (SDD) program.

The committee believes that the F–35 represents an essential national capability. However, it remains concerned about whether the F–35 Joint Strike Fighter program will deliver required capability required by each of the services when the services need it and at prices the Department can afford.

The basis for that concern arises principally from several reviews that were conducted late last year at the direction of the Secretary of Defense, including reviews by the Joint Estimating Team, an Industry Manufacturing Review Team, and a Joint Assessment Team. In their annual assessments of the program, the Director, Operational Testing and Evaluation and the Government Accountability Office (GAO) also conveyed troubling information about the program's ability to perform as promised.

Based on the reviews he directed, the Secretary of Defense fundamentally restructured the program to: (1) extend the development test schedule to March 2015; (2) add additional research, development, testing, and evaluation funds to pay for mitigating known risks; (3) buy another carrier variant developmental test aircraft and add another software integration line to the program; (4) use up to three aircraft procured under low-rate initial production (LRIP) contracts for developmental testing; (5) reduce procurement quantities over the future-years defense program to slow the planned production ramp up and offset added funding for developmental testing; and (6) install a new fee structure that would provide incentives for the contractor team to achieve key performance events and cost goals. While the Marine Corps may delay its initial operational capability date for a few months in 2012, the Navy and the Air Force extended theirs several years to 2016.

The committee supports the Secretary's plan to restructure the F–35 JSF program. However, the committee believes that greater insight into it for Congress and others outside the Department is warranted. To achieve that goal, the committee believes that the Defense Department needs to establish milestones against which we can measure progress of the program.

Therefore, in accordance with the goals set forth by the Program Executive Officer for the program, the committee expects the Department of Defense to manage the F–35 Joint Strike Fighter aircraft program so as to achieve the following milestones by the end of this calendar year:

(1) achieve first flight of the F–35C (carrier variant);

(2) install and operate Block 1.0 software on all flight test aircraft to be delivered this year;

(3) fully implement those recommendations of the Independent Manufacturing Review Team, reflected in its October 2009 report and its follow-on assessment of the Production Integrated Transition Plan, that address manufacturing issues affecting initial production (in particular, those recommendations relating to the global supply chain; parts shortages and change management; first article inspections; test and evaluation;

quantitative management metrics; the reduction of unit recurring flyaway costs; an integrated management plan/integrated management schedule; the completion of an independent schedule risk assessment by the government; and assessments of producibility);

(4) deliver all LRIP Lot I aircraft and all remaining developmental aircraft (except for the additional F–35C test aircraft to be bought with fiscal year 2011 funds) in flyable status with software in Block 1.0 configuration;

(5) deliver 11 test aircraft in flyable status with software in Block 1.0 configuration to Patuxent River Naval Air Station and Edwards Air Force Base;

(6) conduct test flights at a rate of 12 flights per aircraft per month;

(7) complete a minimum of 400 test flights;

(8) deliver at least 3 training aircraft to Eglin Air Force Base; and

(9) capture real-time data from the flight testing of all F–35 JSF developmental aircraft and training aircraft using the F–35 Autonomous Logistics Information System. Such data collection shall be sufficient to support the Department's development of a revised operations and sustainment estimate in the second quarter of fiscal year 2012.

If the program reaches each of those milestones, the committee believes that the program will be in a position to award a fixed-price incentive fee contract no later than the fiscal year 2011 procurement.

The Acting Program Executive Officer in the Joint Program Office and the prime contractor both stipulated that the foregoing milestones are achievable.

The committee expects that the program will achieve these milestones and that, if they are not, the Department of Defense will undertake appropriate action to correct any reason for delays, including (but not limited to) withholding fees.

The recommended provision would look prospectively to measure progress during the remainder of the SDD program. As GAO recommended in its most recent report, "Joint Strike Fighter: Additional Costs and Delays Not Meeting Warfighter Requirements on Time," such a plan should provide criteria and conditions for comparing documented results to expected progressive levels of demonstrated weapon system maturity in relationship to planned increases in future procurement quantities.

The committee believes that the system management plan and matrix required under this section will serve as a useful tool by which Congress can require the Department to explain how increasing levels of demonstrated, quantifiable knowledge about the Joint Strike Fighter program's maturity at annual procurement decision-points justify increased procurement funding and quantities, as the program proceeds to a full-rate procurement decision.

Final Action

As passed, H.R. 6523, the Ike Skelton National Defense Authorization Act For Fiscal Year 2011, did not include program-level detail, so no amount was specified for the F-35 program.

In lieu of a conference report, the House and Senate Armed Services Committees issued a joint explanatory statement regarding H.R. 6523. The joint explanatory statement included the Senate management matrix language shown above.

FY2011 Defense Appropriations Act (S. 3800)

Senate

The Senate Appropriations Committee report accompanying S. 3800[131] discussed the F-35 program at length. Under Procurement Programs, it stated:

> *F-35 Joint Strike Fighter [JSF]*- The Committee supports the F-35 aircraft program and believes that it is an important capability for the Department of Defense and many partner nations. The fiscal year 2011 budget requests $7,686,100,000 for 42 low-rate initial production aircraft. The 42 aircraft in Lot 5 are: 22 Conventional Take Off and Landing [CTOL] aircraft for the Air Force; 13 Short Take Off and Vertical Landing [STOVL] aircraft for the Marine Corps; and 7 Carrier Variant [CV] aircraft for the Navy. The budget also requests $763,200,000 in advance procurement funding for Lot 6, which will include 45 aircraft for the United States and 8 for partner nations.
>
> Realizing that JSF development was taking longer and costing more than planned, the Department of Defense undertook a comprehensive program review last fall. This in-depth evaluation led to the program being restructured in February 2010. The revised plan extends the development phase by 13 months, adds a CV aircraft to the test program, and moves the full rate production decision to fiscal year 2016. The Government-contractor relationship has changed and the production contract for Lot 4 will be a fixed price incentive fee rather than a cost-plus contract vehicle. An Independent Manufacturing Review Team [IMRT], created to evaluate manufacturing, discovered a number of production process weaknesses. The program office and contractor team are working through the IMRT's recommendations to help achieve and sustain production ramp-up. The Committee believes that the Department has moved in the right direction to bring more realistic schedules and costs into focus.
>
> Concerns about progress in the test program and the maturation of the manufacturing process persist. In his June 2010 letter accompanying the Nunn-McCurdy certification documentation, the Under Secretary of Defense (Acquisition, Technology and Logistics) stated that the test program continues to encounter difficulties and has fallen behind the level of performance projected just a few months ago. These challenges to the test program are of particular note for testing of the F-35B STOVL aircraft, which has been set back by late delivery of aircraft to Government test and failures to meet the number of planned test flights.
>
> A recent 'quick look' by the IMRT found significant improvements in risk management plans, change management and global supply but that additional progress was needed in a number of manufacturing areas. Parts shortages, change management processes and first article inspections are the key areas where further steps forward are needed. The Committee is aware that production has not moved as quickly as previously planned and has not kept pace with scheduled ramp rate increases. With Lot 5, the Department will buy its 100th aircraft—yet none of the production aircraft ordered to date have been delivered. The first

---

[131] S.Rept. 111-295.

delivery from Lot 1 (fiscal year 2007) was scheduled for delivery in September 2009; it now appears that it will deliver in December 2010.

The Committee recommends a reduction of 10 aircraft from the fiscal year 2011 (Lot 5) procurement (6 Air Force CTOL, 3 Marine Corps STOVL, and 1 Navy CV). This adjustment reduces the concurrency of development and production, provides time to mature manufacturing processes and institute supply chain improvements, and stabilizes production at the fiscal year 2010 rate for 1 year. The Advance Procurement request is fully funded to sustain the supplier base and implement manufacturing improvements. The budget adjustments are a decrease of $770,000,000 in Aircraft Procurement, Navy and a decrease of $730,200,000 in Aircraft Procurement, Air Force.

In discussion of Research, Development, Testing, and Evaluation, the SAC report continued:

Joint Strike Fighter.—The budget request includes $2,477,041,000 number for development and test of the F-35 Joint Strike Fighter. As a result of the schedule delays and cost increases in the program, the Department of Defense has conducted exhaustive reviews of the program, culminating in a restructuring of the program in February 2010 and a Nunn-McCurdy certification in June 2010. The Committee is encouraged by the addition of aircraft into the flight test program, the revisions to the test schedule, and new fee structures to incentivize contractor performance.

However, the Committee is circumspect on the ability of the Department to complete the revised test program on schedule. Just months after the program restructure, the Under Secretary of Defense (Acquisition, Technology, and Logistics) notified the congressional defense committees on June 1, 2010, that the 'JSF test program continues to encounter difficulties and has fallen behind the level of performance projected' by the Joint Estimating Team II.

Between February and June of this year, for example, the estimated ferry date—the time at which an aircraft becomes available for Government testing—has been delayed for 8 out of 14 test aircraft by as much as 2 months. In addition, the Marine Corps' short take-off and landing variant has not met the scheduled ramp-up of flight testing due to maintenance and other issues. Due to the under-execution of test flights, the Committee recommends a reduction of $50,000,000 to the Research, Development, Test and Evaluation, Navy account.

The Department has also requested a total of $115,724,000 for development of Block 4 software. This software is intended to have enhancements beyond the Block 3 build, which will be installed on all operational aircraft after completion of the developmental test program in fiscal year 2014. In light of the considerable risk remaining in the test schedule, the Committee recommendation defers all funds requested for initiating development of Block 4 software.

The overall performance of the F-35 program was also discussed in a section of the SAC report entitled "Restoring Budget Discipline":

Most disturbing perhaps is the Joint Strike Fighter [JSF]. For the last 3 years in conference, this Committee has insisted on fully funding the JSF in conjunction with providing funds to develop a second engine for the program. This approach was in accord with the stated position of the administration that it would not object to Congress supporting the second engine if its funding did not come at the expense of the overall JSF program. While the second engine program has continued its development on track, with the program being awarded 17 straight performance awards in the past 8 years with an average approval rating of 93.5 percent, the JSF has seen cost increases and significant delays. In fact at the end of

June 2010, 9 months after the start of the fiscal year, the program maintained unobligated balances of $6,500,000,000. This amount for 1 year's production funding of this program is more than the budgets of many entire Federal agencies.

Despite the nearly unwavering congressional support of the JSF program, the delivery of the first two production aircraft has slipped by an additional year, and the cost of the program has continued to increase. It is clear that the aircraft sought for fiscal year 2011 will not begin production until at the earliest the end of the coming fiscal year. The importance of the JSF program and the urgent need to replace aging fighters is the sole reason why the Committee is only scaling back production and not recommending eliminating all funding for this program for fiscal year 2011. The incongruence of the insistence on canceling the second engine program which has been a near model program and which most analysts expect would curtail long-term costs of the entire JSF program with equal insistence on the need to fully fund the JSF program is hard to rationalize.

Final Action

In lieu of a defense appropriations bill, the House and Senate passed a series of continuing resolutions maintaining spending at FY2010 levels from October 1, 2010, through April 15, 2011.

FY2011 DOD and Full-Year Continuing Appropriations Act

The FY2011 Department of Defense and Full-Year Continuing Appropriations Act (H.R. 1473), signed into law on April 15, 2011, provided DOD funding for the remainder of FY2011. Significant changes in F-35 funding in the act include

- Cutting 10 F-35Bs, saving $1.7 billion, of which $974 million was transferred to Aircraft Procurement, Air Force for eight additional F-35As.

- Cutting $608.5M for five F-35As, for a net increase of three aircraft over the Administration request.

- Cutting a total of $116.5M from all F-35 models for funding carryovers.

- Transferring $29.7M from the F-35A modification line to F-35A procurement per Air Force request.

Taken in sum, F-35-related actions in the FY2011 Department of Defense and Full-Year Continuing Appropriations Act totaled a reduction of $2.16 billion from the Administration request.

Appendix B. F-35 Key Performance Parameters

Table B-1 summarizes key performance parameters for the three versions of the F-35.

Table B-1. F-35 Key Performance Parameters (KPPs)

Source of KPP	KPP	F-35A Air Force CTOL version	F-35B Marine Corps STOVL version	F-35C Navy carrier-suitable version
Joint	Radio frequency signature	Very low observable	Very low observable	Very low observable
	Combat radius	590 nm Air Force mission profile	450 nm Marine Corps mission profile	600 nm Navy mission profile
	Sortie generation	3 surge / 2 sustained	4 surge / 3 sustained	3 surge / 2 sustained
	Logistics footprint	< 8 C-17 equivalent loads (24 PAA)	< 8 C-17 equivalent loads (20 PAA)	< 46,000 cubic feet, 243 short tons
	Mission reliability	93%	95%	95%
	Interoperability	Meet 100% of critical, top-level information exchange requirements; secure voice and data		
Marine Corps	STOVL mission performance – short-takeoff distance	n/a	550 feet	n/a
	STOVL mission performance – vertical lift bring-back	n/a	2 x 1K JDAM, 2 x AIM-120, with reserve fuel	n/a
Navy	Maximum approach speed	n/a	n/a	145 knots

Source: F-35 program office, October 11, 2007.

Notes: PAA is primary authorized aircraft (per squadron); vertical lift bring back is the amount of weapons with which plane can safely land.

Author Contact Information

Jeremiah Gertler
Specialist in Military Aviation
jgertler@crs.loc.gov, 7-5107

www.ingramcontent.com/pod-product-compliance
Lightning Source LLC
Chambersburg PA
CBHW080614290526
45790CB00007B/2778